HISTORIC TEXAS
a photographic portrait

Otis and Iris Davis, with their sons, William and Paul.
Unidentified photographer.

HISTORIC TEXAS
a photographic portrait

MARTHA A. SANDWEISS, GENERAL EDITOR
ROY FLUKINGER, ASSOCIATE EDITOR
ANNE W. TUCKER, CONTRIBUTING EDITOR

ESSAY BY WILLIAM A. OWENS

PICTURE RESEARCH AND CAPTIONS BY
RICHARD PEARCE-MOSES

TEXAS MONTHLY PRESS

All photographs used by permission.

Essay copyright 1986 by William A. Owens.

Copyright 1986 Texas Historical Foundation. All rights including reproduction by photographic or electronic process and translation into other languages are fully reserved under the International Copyright Union, the Universal Copyright Convention, and the Pan-American Copyright Convention. Reproduction or use of this book in whole or in part in any manner without written permission of the publisher is strictly prohibited.

Texas Monthly Press, Inc.
P.O. Box 1569
Austin, Texas 78767

A B C D E F G H

Library of Congress Cataloging-in-Publication Data

Main entry under title:

Historic Texas.

   Includes index.
   1. Texas—Description and travel—Views.
2. Texas—History—Pictorial works. 3. Texas—
Biography—Portraits. I. Owens, William A.,
1905–   . II. Pearce-Moses, Richard.
III. Sandweiss, Martha A. IV. Texas Historical
Foundation.
F387.H59 1986   976.4   85-12571
ISBN 0-87719-021-6

Printed in Japan by Dai Nippon Printing Co. Ltd. through DNP (America), Inc.

Design by The Smitherman Corporation

*This book is an outgrowth
of the
Texas Photography Project,
a program of the
Texas Historical Foundation
made possible by a generous grant
from the
Du Pont Company and Conoco,
its energy subsidiary.*

contents

Historic Texas: A Photographic Portrait 9	1900's 121
Texas Places, Texas Faces 13	1910's 147
	1920's 171
	1930's 193
	1940's 225
Pre-1869 43	1950's 261
1870's 55	1960's 283
1880's 69	1970's 299
1890's 91	Picture Credits 319

historic texas

This is a book of Texan photographs; that is, photographs made in and about Texas. Photography and Texas are about the same age. The invention of the daguerreotype, the first really practical photographic process, was announced in 1839, three years after Texas became a republic and six years before it became a state. The earliest picture in this book dates from 1853; the last from 1980. Yet this is not an illustrated history of the state or an evenhanded history of regional photography. It is simply a book of pictures that seemed compelling to the editors. Some pictures engaged our interest because they documented a particular event in the history of Texas, but a great many more attracted us because they said something about uncelebrated lives or uncelebrated places that, taken as a whole, suggest the fabric of Texas life; a life that, as William Owens points out in his essay, has been resolutely diverse.

We did not include pictures of Great Texans unless we liked the pictures. Similarly, we did not include images by Great Photographers unless the pictures also seemed to say something of interest about life in Texas. Because we sought descriptive pictures, we excluded abstract photographs, formal still lifes, and more experimental works that did not, in some way, describe the state. Because of publishing constraints we had to exclude many fine color pictures. Nonetheless, we feel we have a book that celebrates the vitality of the photographic medium as well as the vitality of Texas life.

This book and its companion volume, *Contemporary Texas: A Photographic Portrait*, have been produced under the auspices of the Texas Historical Foundation which, as part of its broader photography programs, is also overseeing the compilation of a guide to all photographic collections and archives in the state of Texas and the publication of a directory of nineteenth-century photographers in Texas. The foundation's share of proceeds from these books will go back into its photography programs and to a special restoration fund for the state capitol building. Richard Pearce-Moses, who is directing the photography programs, did all of the work to assemble the pictures for this book. He went through hundreds of snapshots sent to his office by people who read about the project. And with enormous energy (and a small computer, camera, and copystand in the back of his car) he drove more than 12,000 miles back and forth across Texas, visiting libraries, historical societies, private collectors, newspaper morgues, museums, and municipal archives. He looked at hundreds of thousands of photographs and made thousands of copies for reference purposes. Back in Austin, Roy Flukinger, Curator of the Photography Collection at the Harry Ransom Humanities Research Center, University of Texas at Austin, and Anne W. Tucker, Gus and Lyndall Wortham Curator, Works on Paper, for the Museum of Fine Arts in Houston, and I went through these copy prints and picked out the 360 pictures reproduced here.

A project like this is inevitably a collaborative effort. Special thanks go to Lawrence T. Jones, who generously allowed us to use images from his outstanding private collection and assisted with numerous research queries, and to David Haynes at the Institute of Texan Cultures, who provided much information about the photographers represented here. All of the staff members at the collections we consulted also deserve thanks, with particular mention going to Tom Sheldon of the Institute of Texan Cultures and Martha Utterback of the Library of the Daughters of the Republic of Texas at the Alamo.

Many of the photographers whose pictures we wished to use graciously waived their reproduction fees, so that this book could be a more profitable fund-raiser for the Texas Historical Foundation. We are grateful to them for their double contribution to this project.

Important support for this book came from Governor Mark White, and our thanks go to him and his staff for their interest and their efforts at publicizing the project.

Additional counsel for this book has come from Frank Calhoun, Russell Lee, Archie McDonald, Brux Austin, Lynn Barnett, and John Ben Shepperd.

At the Texas Historical Foundation, we've received much help from Executive Director Leon

Lurie and his predecessor Morrison Parrott, and from staff members Joanne Deaver, Tanya Fain, and Mark Trowbridge.

If any one person can be said to be responsible for a project that has involved as many people as this, it is undoubtedly William P. Wright, Jr. A member of the Texas Historical Foundation Board since 1978 and Vice-President since 1983, Bill has been the driving force behind all of the foundation's photographic programs. The idea of producing this book of photographs of Texas to celebrate the state's sesquicentennial was his, and no one who met him and encountered his great enthusiasm could ever doubt that the project would be done.

Our final thanks go to the Du Pont Company and Conoco, its energy subsidiary, for their very generous support of the Texas Historical Foundation's photography projects. Their grant has made it possible for the foundation to publish this book and its companion volume of contemporary Texas images and to do the research for a guide to Texas photo archives. At the Du Pont Company and Conoco, its energy subsidiary, Constantine Nicandros, Gary Edwards, E. L. Lively, Ben Boldt, Perry McCahill, Eric Oshlo, Loretta Pittman, and Tom DeCola have been of particular assistance, and Sondra Fowler has been of great help publicizing our search for photographs. In every regard, the support of the Du Pont Company and Conoco, its energy subsidiary, has been a sterling example of enlightened cooperation between a corporation and a non-profit organization. We are all indebted to the people of the Du Pont Company and Conoco, its energy subsidiary, for their interest in Texas, their enthusiasm for photography, and their support of a project like this, which we hope will be enjoyed by people throughout Texas and everywhere.

Martha A. Sandweiss
Curator of Photographs, Amon Carter Museum
General Editor

images
texas places, texas faces

In 1782, from his farmhouse near West Point, New York, J. Hector St. John de Crèvecoeur, a French emigré, asked a question relevant then and no less relevant now: "What then is the American, this new man?" His answer then is still convincing enough now for me to apply it to the Texan today: "He is either an European, or the descendant of an European, hence that strange mixture of blood, which you will find in no other country. I could point out to you a family whose grandfather was an Englishman, whose wife was Dutch, whose son married a French woman, and whose present four sons have now four wives of different nations." In keeping with the accepted prejudice of his time de Crèvecoeur omitted non-Europeans such as American Indians and Afro-American slaves.

With the change of one word I have made his question applicable to our time and place: "What then is the Texan, this new man?" The obvious answer is that he, too, is an American with strains of European blood in his veins. The difference is that collectively the Texan is inheritor of blood mixtures not known or acceptable in de Crèvecoeur's time. As an observer de Crèvecoeur was restricted culturally and geographically. While he was collecting impressions along the Atlantic seaboard from Boston to Charleston, western frontiersmen had reached the Ohio River and turned southward into Kentucky.

It is possible that he had knowledge of Americans as diverse in character as the New England peddler, the Pennsylvania farmer, and the Scotch-Irish gamecock of the wilderness. Notwithstanding the limits of his knowledge he derived a theory original and far-reaching—that America would become a melting pot, an amalgam of all blood strains, all cultures as he had observed them. Intellectually, if not emotionally, his theory promised for the future easing of tensions in a society already pluralistic. Even in his life-time racial and religious conflicts flawed his ideal, but it remained a perennial dream in the minds of social optimists.

Nearly two centuries after de Crèvecoeur published his *Letters from an American Farmer* I used it as the starting point for *A Fair and Happy Land*, an informal narrative of the American frontier, put together from census records, land records, court records, printed local histories, and the vast amount of pioneer experience accumulated in the often poignant "they say" of countless men and women who made the long trek from the Atlantic seaboard to east Texas. Again I find it useful as I attempt to explore the Texas character and many-faced Texas culture, this time with indispensable photographs, some of my own family.

Born November 2, 1905, in Pin Hook, Lamar County, Texas, I have lived in awareness of half of Texas history, and in shadowy memories of the other half from vivid recollections as they came to me in song and story. I was born forty years after Appomattox and twenty-five years after the last dispersion of the Comanches, both watersheds of history in the minds of people I grew up among. For more than half of my life I have diligently studied Texas land, Texas people, Texas culture as they appeared to me among diverse ethnic groups, in diverse settings.

As diligently, I sought ways of telling as diverse as the substance of history I found among the people. In a letter from Roy Bedichek to Walter Prescott Webb, dated February 15, 1951, I discovered eminent men wrestling with the problem: "There should be no hesitation about using the personal pronoun. It consists of one letter, is the center and axle of the whole universe, and it is an affectation to avoid it. . . . Nothing else so humanizes writing, and certainly historical writing needs humanizing."

My purpose here is to share impressions, not through formal history or any other discipline but by recounting where we came from, what intermixings happened along the way, by what names we call ourselves. Though not footnoted it is true—not in every instance verifiable truth but the truth of human experience recorded in the vicarious "they say" of generation after generation, a truth substantiated in treasured photographs that record who they were and where they lived. In the knowledge that countless numbers of early settlers in Texas had frontier experiences parallel with those of my family, I present the latter as general and symbolic.

In life span Jane Witherspoon, my great-great-

Jane Edmonds Witherspoon and Mary Elizabeth Hall Backus. *Unidentified photographer.* From a copy print of a carte-de-visite. Eagle Pass, Maverick County, early 1860s. Collection of Oscar Backus.

grandmother, goes farthest back in time and widest in spaces traveled. She was born Jane Edmunds May 10, 1800, to an English family living in tidewater Virginia. A part of the early westward movement, her family crossed the Alleghenies, probably through the Cumberland Gap, and settled at Bowling Green, Kentucky. In 1819 she married Wiley Witherspoon, who was also born in Virginia, who also had crossed the Alleghenies and traveled down westward-flowing rivers. Indications are that he was descended from Witherspoons who lived in Yester Parish, Haddington, Midlothian County, Scotland, the parish in which John the Signer preached as a young man. At an unknown date they traveled a newly opened migration route across the Ohio, Indiana, the Mississippi, and probably on to Potosi, Missouri, territory acquired in the Louisiana Purchase. Their first child, Catherine, my great-grandmother, was born in Missouri or Arkansas.

In 1834 they received from the Mexican government a grant of two leagues of land and settled at what became Pin Hook on Little Pine Creek. With the help of Negro slaves they built their home on an Indian mound on land that had been cleared by Indians, probably not by the Caddoes as they had long since left the area, but possibly by Delawares, Kickapoos, or Cherokees—tribes who claimed hunting grounds in east Texas. Indians on their way to and from the Red River Crossing at Pine Bluff passed their place, and there was some Indian trouble but no stories of raids or scalpings were handed down.

Three more daughters, Martha, Artha Ann, and Mary Ann, were born at Pin Hook. Catherine married John Mason Hall, who was born in New York City, and by him had daughters Mary Elizabeth, Artha Ann, and Harriet. He died about 1850 and lies in an unmarked grave in the Witherspoon family cemetery. In 1856 Catherine married William Duval from Kentucky and by him had daughters Melinda and Lizer.

In December 1849, *The Northern Standard*, in nearby Clarksville, published a story about the Gold Rush in California. Wiley Witherspoon was fifty-four, Jane fifty, but in spite of their ages they apparently caught the California fever. In January 1850, they deeded their land and livestock to their daughter, Catherine Hall, and signed the deeds with their marks.

I could find nothing more about them at Pin Hook. I did learn that a wagon train probably from Missouri came through on the way to California by way of Chihuahua, Mexico, and the Gila River. In May 1850, Jane Witherspoon bought lots in Eagle Pass. Wiley may have died on the way. The story does not end there.

About the end of the Civil War Mary Elizabeth Hall went to join her grandmother Witherspoon in Eagle Pass. April 6, 1870, she married Joseph Backus, a German emigré from Alsace-Lorraine. Ulysses Joseph, their son, was born February 8, 1871. Mary Elizabeth Backus died January 3, 1906. December 29, 1906, Ulysses, Episcopalian, graduate of Texas A&M, married Mary Esther Valdez, Roman Catholic and Mexican.

Jane Witherspoon died in 1890 in Eagle Pass after the long journey from the Atlantic to the Rio Grande. Among the legacies she left me I treasure none more than the cousins, descendants of Ulysses and Esther, completely bilingual, completely bicultural, themselves a contribution to my search for *the Texan*.

My other family photographs have parallel stories. In one my father, whom I never saw, stands straight and firm, as all my life I have imagined him to have been—an image I have often turned to for nearly eighty years, that and the meager knowledge that he was second-generation Welsh and was born in Indiana.

Seated next to him is Missouri Ann Cleaver, a great-grandmother who lived with my family at the time. Though I was only two when she died her life story remained with me very much alive: She had Dutch blood; she was born in 1833, the year she said the stars fell on Alabama; in Arkansas she was arrested by Union soldiers and accused of being a Confederate spy. When my need to know had to be satisfied I set out to find whether these were true or made-up stories. In Germantown, Pennsylvania, I found records of Cleavers with a mixture of English and Dutch blood. There was also evidence that William Cleaver, her great-grandfather, had gone west about 1770, perhaps traveling as far as Winchester, Virginia, in a Conestoga wagon. In the excitement of this discovery I was impelled to follow his trail and did—over the rugged Allegheny Front and down to the Tygart's River Valley, where William and his sons, colonials, fought Indian allies of the British and made cattle drives to supply Washington and his troops in Pennsylvania. In 1779 Quakers with the Boone family in Pennsylvania, they followed Daniel into Kentucky and settled in Nelson County. In the way of frontiersmen the older generation died there; younger generations moved on. I fol-

images

Chennault family portrait. *R. A. Russell* (active 1880s).
From a copy print. Detroit, Red River County, about 1880. Collection of Doris Houchen.
Standing: Eliza Chennault Martin, Franklin Lemmon (son of Julie Ann), Alice Chennault Hignight, Celie Chennault Tippitt. Seated: Andrew Jackson Chennault, Julie Ann Cox Chennault.

lowed Stephen Cleaver, Missouri Ann's grandfather, to Frankfort, Missouri, near Hannibal, where he was elected delegate and served in framing the Missouri constitution.

In 1826, Stephen's son Henry, Missouri Ann's father, moved south to Alabama. There he married Nancy Ann Coleman, whose family had come by wagon train from Spartanburg, South Carolina. There at Cleaver Hill, not far from Selma, in that fabled time, Missouri Ann was born. With whites and blacks together she was made to believe that the shower of stars bore a gift of magic, in her mind not to be used as a curse but as a reading of signs light or dark of what would befall.

In 1826 Henry Cleaver took his family, slaves, and livestock across the Mississippi and for the second time turned a part of the wilderness into a productive plantation, this time near Camden, Arkansas. History allotted him fifteen years to establish himself and his three sons, three daughters before the Civil War came with its disruption of life, its sudden attack on body and soul at home and on the battlefield. Jesse Herndon James, Missouri Ann's husband, left her and their four small children to build wagons for the Confederate army. He died of sunstroke. The war came closer. The Battle of Poison Springs was so close to Missouri Ann's house that bullets rattled on walls and roof, with a sound that Martha Alice James, my grandmother, described until it was part of my recollection.

The war having left Missouri Ann destitute, she loaded her children and the belongings she had left and set out on a journey that ended at Pin Hook.

In the third photograph the seated man is Andrew Jackson Chennault, brother of Aaron, Martha Alice's husband, my grandfather. I have been told that they were descendants of French Huguenots. Records show that they were born near Salem, Illinois, the town of Abraham Lincoln's youth. They moved to Arkansas in time to serve in the Confederate army. The woman in the front row is Julie Cox Chennault, by blood part Cherokee, pure Indian to me in my childhood.

Through all these journeys, where they lived and how they lived, through all these experiences of lives directly or indirectly a part of my own, through photographs in albums or hanging on a wall, I have long felt it imperative to know and understand these Europeans turned American, to comprehend the myths and legends they brought with them, to appreciate the minglings of the old and the new as they transformed the wilderness into their New Ca-

Owens family portrait. *Unidentified photographer.*

From a copy print. Pin Hook (also known as Faulkner), Lamar County, about 1900. Collection of Doris Houchen.

Standing: Alice James Chennault, Charles Owens. Seated: Jessie Ann Chennault Owens holding Dewey Owens, Monroe Owens, Willis McGeehee, Missouri Ann Cleaver James.

naan. Predominantly Anglo-Saxon, predominantly Protestant, dissenters from any established church, frontiersmen outside the law of any episcopacy, believers that the Bible was the word of God and the only word of God—they took the myth of the Promised Land literally. To them, the land that was America was theirs and they had the God-given right to possess it no matter from whom they wrested it.

It was their sons and daughters and generations of other sons and daughters who led the way west as wave after wave of pioneers climbed the Allegheny Front, hacked their way through wilderness thickets to the Cumberland Gap, followed westward-flowing rivers till they knew they had found the right stopping place, a place that provided wood and water and tillable land. Whether on a legal survey or a tree-slashed "tomahawk claim," they built first their brush lean-tos and later their log cabins, some with half-chimneys, like the one Abraham Lincoln was born in. Schools and churches slow a-building, puncheon-floored homes echoed to the *a b ab* of a spelling class or a call to the Cross of a self-ordained itinerant preacher.

No matter how far west they went, settlers clung to vestiges of what they had inherited from Europe. The Bible was their literature, hymns from Isaac Watts and John Newton were their comfort, English and Scottish ballads and the sawing of a catgut fiddle their entertainment. As clothes brought from older settlements wore out, men and women learned from Indians how to dress in doeskin. Such life, especially on fringes of the frontier, made the settlers rugged, individualistic, violent in Indian escapades, at times violent among themselves. As time passed they handed down images of the realities of their lives: the log cabin for shelter, the long rifle for protection, the raccoon cap for warmth. By the time the pioneers settled west of the Alleghenies the backbone and ribs of American culture were in place. Settlers in new regions or from different ethnic groups could add to but not change the structure.

When I could no longer follow the trails of my kin, when again I studied their faces in the photographs, I knew how indelible on my mind was the long frontier trek, the unmarked graves alongside trails—on my mind and the minds of Texans consciously or unconsciously. At the same time I knew that what had been passed on to me was an inheritance from a distant past imported from old countries but barnacled by bits and pieces out of the

images

westering experience.

In the sixth grade at Pin Hook, as prescribed by state law, I studied Texas history. As the teacher had been taught he taught us in a patriotic glow bordering on chauvinism. Texas was big, bigger than any other state, with a history unmatched and unmatchable. What other state had statesmen like Stephen F. Austin and Sam Houston, or heroes who died defending the Alamo—with names like Davy Crockett, William B. Travis, James Bowie, James Butler Bonham? In the teacher's rote method we memorized names and details of battles. When we came to the defeat at the Alamo his voice became reverent; at the Battle of San Jacinto he boasted that Santa Anna deserved his fate.

Eight years later, teaching in the Pin Hook school, I taught Texas history to the sixth grade as he had taught it to me, except that I dwelled longer on the Neutral Ground and the first settlers, using details from memory, adding details learned away from Pin Hook, largely as they followed there.

In their hunger for land Anglo-Saxons, my kin among them, pushed west and then farther west, driving the Indians before them, trading beads and trinkets for land when they could, fighting for it when they could not. All the way they were aided, sometimes by the colonial, more generally by the United States government. By the Treaty of Paris in 1783, the end of the Revolution, the United States acquired from Great Britain the territory west to the Mississippi and south to Florida—from the British but not from the Indians. In the Louisiana Purchase in 1803 the United States acquired from the French but not the Indians the territory extending from the Mississippi to the Rocky Mountains—an expanse that doubled the size of the United States. Because terms of the purchase did not define exact boundaries, the United States laid claim to the part of the territory that became Texas. Spain disputed the claim. In 1806 representatives of the two countries reached the agreement that neither would govern the strip of land between the Arroyo Hondo and the Sabine River. Soon called the Neutral Ground, this strip became a haven for renegades of various kinds, and among them Anglos (the term that came into general use) on their way to Texas, determined to breach the border and grab the riches that lay before them.

By then Spain was beginning to lose control of Mexico, a control invalidated in September 1821, when Mexican revolutionaries rose against Spain and secured their independence. Under the Mexican Republic the vast territory called Tejas by the Indians, Texas by the Anglos, was vulnerable to encroachment because of weak rule from Mexico City and uncontrolled borders north and east. Renegades and unlawful settlers unchecked crossed over from the Neutral Ground and at Red River crossings.

During the same time organized immigration became a fact. In 1820 Moses Austin, an enterprising Yankee who had tried various parts of the American frontier, persuaded Spanish authorities to grant him the privilege to settle three hundred families in Texas, a considerable privilege. Each married man was to be allotted 4,600 acres. Austin died in 1821, before the settlement could be established. His son, Stephen F., took up the grant and in 1822 settled a colony on the Gulf of Mexico between the Brazos and Colorado rivers. Some restrictions imposed by the Mexicans were galling, some merely to be winked at. Each man had to be certified by Austin that he was a Mexican citizen, a Roman Catholic, and a person of good character.

In spite of these restrictions other *empresarios* negotiated grants, among them Sterling C. Robertson and Hayden Edwards, whose grants would eventually create bloody conflict between Anglos and Cherokees. Impatient with the *empresario* system, would-be settlers waited in Arkansas and Louisiana for a chance to sneak in. Following practices learned on older frontiers, squatters who got in moved on until they found land that looked like the land they had left, staked out claims, marked the claims with slashes on trees, cleared the land, built on it, all without a by-your-leave from Mexican authorities, confident in the belief that there was plenty of time to survey and receive a parchment deed.

Early migration was chiefly overland, though boats from river and Atlantic ports put settlers ashore on Galveston Island and other points on the Texas Gulf shore. Those who preferred to could follow old trails cleared by French and Spanish explorers and traders. Of these the most frequently traveled was the *Camino Real* from New Orleans to San Antonio by way of Natchitoches and Nacogdoches.

The main overland routes, routes traveled by various members of my family, though often meandering, at some time veered to and through the South. Whichever meandering these settlers took they were more than brushed with southern culture and southern sympathy. Any analysis of the Texas character or the Texas culture must take into consideration the fact that, though early census

records are unreliable, the census of 1860 indicates that perhaps as many as one hundred Southerners to one non-Southerner had entered before the Civil War. Of these Southerners, as early as 1830 three cultural strains were discernible: the plantation owner of the lowland, the poor white farmer of the upland, and the Afro-American slave.

Plantation owners in the main would have been at home with the *Book of Common Prayer* in Bruton Parish. Some of their sons would have read law at the University of Virginia; others would have taken up the study of medicine in New Orleans. Plantation owners traveled in covered wagon trains, the women and children riding inside, the men and boys on horseback, the slaves able to walk walking, taking care of the horses, herding the cattle. Near rich bottom lands, as in Calvert, plantation owners built homes in imitation of plantations they had left behind and furnished them with silver and furniture befitting a Georgian or Greek revival. For their slaves they built cabins of notched poles, the spaces between chinked with slivers of wood and daubed with clay.

Poor white settlers from the red hills of Georgia, Alabama, and Mississippi traveled when they could in ox carts sheltered by a canvas wagon sheet, or they came on horseback or walking, traveling the long miles on shank's mare, as they called it. Trees were their first shelters, and then arbors made of poles and branches and leaves as a make-do till they could build something better. Eventually three styles became common: the shotgun, two or three rooms, one behind the other; the one-room plank with a lean-to porch in front, a lean-to kitchen at the back; the two pens with a dog-trot hall between and a porch—gallery they called it—across the front.

Rich or poor, white or black, vulgar or refined, they brought vestiges of language traceable to Queen Anne's reign but in phraseology obscured by layers of hillbilly singsong and African timbre and rhythm; they brought vestiges as well of European music in church song, ballad, and fiddle tune, with occasional blurring as the melodies were picked up by slaves in field or cabin. It was a hybrid culture, born of two hundred years of mingling, chiefly white to black, with occasional but rarely acknowledged mixed blood. From master to slave, work was an ethic drawn from the Bible—an ethic that drove them to clear and plant this part of the wilderness.

In the South, cotton had been king, whether on a plantation or a poor-white farm. Cotton became king in this new land as fast as it could be cleared and planted. Even in the time of the *empresarios* the kingdom was gradually expanding up the Red River into the cross-timbers, and at the same time in the bottoms along the Trinity, Brazos, and Colorado. Two southern images became common—the cotton chopper swinging his hoe in the spring, the cotton picker dragging his cotton sack or basket in the fall. Images of cotton towns were greeted as signs of progress—the cotton gin with a line of cotton wagons waiting, the cotton yard where buyers graded lint—short staple, long staple—and paid by quality and weight the money that made the place a town.

As the first *empresario* Stephen F. Austin had set high standards for settlers in his colony: "No frontiersman who has no occupation than that of a hunter will be received. No drunkard, nor gambler, nor profane idler, nor any man against whom there is even probable ground of suspicion that he is a bad man." Other *empresarios*, of whom there were a number, were less strict in selecting settlers they admitted and less scrupulous in regard to boundaries of claims already settled by Anglos or Indians. These, Austin would have called undesirables. Worse were the settlers who, with few if any scruples, crossed borders at will and took the land they wanted.

In 1825 Mexican officials opened Texas to free colonization, a generous gesture they soon regretted as thousands of immigrants took up land faster than claims could be processed. Understandably, Mexicans decided that all Anglos were undesirables—aggressive, knavish land-grabbers. April 6, 1830, the Mexican congress passed a law excluding admission to all American citizens. This measure was joined to two others: one to annex Texas to the Mexican state Coahuila to facilitate governmental control, the other to encourage resettlement of Mexican citizens on Texas land. Anglos were angered at what they considered a double breach of contract, but they knew they were land-grabbers, as they admitted in a joke handed down: "Texans ain't land greedy. They jes' want what touches their'n."

These measures only exposed more clearly the weakness of the Mexican government. Anglos continued to enter in numbers; few Mexican citizens resettled among the Anglos. Adversary positions developing over land exacerbated Anglo feeling over cultural differences. Language was a major problem; so was religion. Anglo Protestants chafed at having to declare themselves Roman Catholics,

even if in name only. Though what they considered the shadow of Rome hung over them officially, neither preacher nor congregation would tolerate a cross or any other religious sign or symbol in their churches. Those who displayed them were Mexican, idolatrous, to be looked down on. For three centuries there had been a gradual mingling of Spanish blood and culture with Indian blood and culture, the result in Anglo prejudice a hybrid inferior to both. In any case, because Mexican settlements were in Nacogdoches, San Antonio, and toward the Rio Grande, few confrontations developed. Even token mixing of Anglo and Mexican would take a century or more, two wars, and bloodshed on both sides. Prejudice dies a lingering death.

The Texas Revolution, inevitable as the Mexicans forced a tighter hold and Anglos rebelled at any hold, was a short time a-brewing, and the fighting time shorter. As in the American Revolution, customs collectors began harassing the colonists and the colonists harassing the collectors. Arrogance prevailed on both sides, arrogance and defiance. Throughout Texas, colonists began holding protest meetings and urging independence. In Mexico, amid internal turmoil, Antonio Lopez de Santa Anna, a defacto dictator, dismissed the legislature of Coahuila and Texas and assembled an army to march north against the Anglos.

October 2, 1835, a hastily picked-up band of volunteers defeated a Mexican force at Gonzales. A soldier named Smithwick accurately characterized men in that fight as well as volunteers in groups assembling under self-appointed officers; "I cannot remember that there was any distinct understanding as to the position we were to assume toward Mexico. Some were for independence, some for the Constitution of 1824, and some for anything, just so it was a row. But we were all ready to fight."

In spite of what Smithwick had to say, in the period between October 2, 1835, and April 21, 1836, the future of Texas as an independent nation was in balance, with the weight heavy in favor of Mexico. It was also the period in which the founding myths and legends had their beginning—in battles fought and a hardening position against the Mexican government and army. Dates and actions are indicative of the Texan passion for freedom.

October 9, 1835, fifty volunteers captured the fort at Goliad; October 28 soldiers under the command of James Bowie and James W. Fannin, Jr., defeated four hundred Mexicans near San Antonio; November 3 citizens met at San Felipe and adopted a provisional government; Sam Houston issued a call for volunteers from the United States; Stephen F. Austin issued a proclamation: "War is our only recourse."

December 9 a detachment under the command of Ben Milam took San Antonio, and settlers thought the war was over. But the balance was shifting to the Mexicans. General Santa Anna was assembling a large army to renew the fight. February 23, 1836, he was ready to attack the Alamo. The defenders, under the command of William B. Travis and James Bowie, numbered fewer than two hundred, hardly a match for the Mexicans. March 6, at daybreak, the Mexicans attacked. When the cannons were silenced one hundred and eighty-seven Texans were dead. March 2 delegates meeting at Washington-on-the-Brazos signed the Declaration of Independence. March 27, Palm Sunday, Santa Anna's soldiers subdued the garrison at Goliad, marched the defenders out, and gunned them down.

April 21, after minor maneuvers, General Sam Houston, his soldiers shouting "Remember the Alamo! Remember Goliad!" charged Santa Anna and his troops at their siesta. Houston reported that the battle lasted eighteen minutes. That was the final battle. The people of Texas were free, free to fly their chosen symbol, the Lone Star flag, free to call themselves Texans.

Out of the nimbus, as in wars throughout history, Texans cherished the myth and enhanced it with legends of battles lost or won, of heroes who fought courageously, some to die bravely, the fallen at the Alamo to be honored in a shrine that is the Alamo. Single-minded, secure in the uniqueness of the history that is their own, Texans have drawn lines of demarcation between themselves and a less favored world, and celebrated their oneness in painting, story, and song.

At the time the Anglos gained their independence they had been living for almost a score of years under Mexican rule but not dominated by Mexican culture. Because of distances there was little rubbing of shoulders. There were small Mexican communities around Nacogdoches and Anahuac, but the larger ones were at Gonzales, Goliad, San Antonio, and south to the Rio Grande. Anglos had little use for things Mexican except the Spanish guitar, and it had already penetrated earlier frontiers.

Mixing of Anglo and Cherokee blood and culture seemed a more likely prospect. Their paths had crossed in many ways in the South, where the

images

Cherokees were considered a civilized tribe. Sam Houston had spent much of his youth with Cherokees who adopted him and gave him the name "The Raven." Among them was the Bowle, also called Chief Bowles, a man strong in character, as was Houston. The two were destined to play out their parts in a tragedy they both tried to avoid, a tragedy linked with the forced removal of the Cherokees from the southern states to the Indian territory—a removal so heartless as to be called "The Trail of Tears."

The Cherokees under Chief Bowles were doomed to the same. In 1819 Spanish officials granted Bowles a tract of land between the Neches and Sabine rivers, but the wording was ambiguous. Mexican officials granted land to Anglos that encroached on Cherokee land. The Chief turned to his friend President Sam Houston. Houston promised that the boundary lines would be honored. But against the greed of Anglo land speculators his efforts were in vain. The Indians would have to go. Not to make amends but in friendship Houston gave the Chief a military cap, scarlet military jacket, and sword.

In June 1839, President Mirabeau B. Lamar ordered the removal of the Cherokees to Indian territory. Chief Bowles defied the order and both sides began preparing for a fight. July 16, 1839, after a day of skirmishing, the Texans came upon Cherokee warriors near the Neches River. Chief Bowles, then about eighty-four years old, wearing Houston's hat and vest and carrying his sword, led the counterattack. In the midst of bloody battle the Chief's horse was shot from under him. As he tried to walk away he was shot in the back. He fell but managed to pull himself up into a sitting position. A Texan's bullet through his head killed him instantly. The Battle of the Neches over, the remaining Cherokees, after hours of mourning, slipped away in the night and crossed the Red River at Pine Bluff. The Chief's military hat, vest, and sword were returned to a bitter Sam Houston.

At the beginning of 1840, with the Indians driven out, two ethnic groups dominated in east Texas: Anglo and Afro, master and slave, both locked in circumstances that enforced cultural sharing, unrepressed, provocative, and creative, in patterns passed generation to generation for a hundred years. Farming had been their way of life as they migrated stop by stop across the Southland. Farming was their way of life as they spread farther west, often with master and slave and hired white man working in the field side by side from daylight to dark. In freshly cleared new ground they planted corn for food and forage, and cotton for cash as it had always been in the South. Cotton, with its domination of life from May to December, brought Anglo and Afro so close together that one from the other subliminally absorbed words, tunes, rhythms. Chopping or picking, all hands, all ages, went to the field, where one might pray another's "Oh, Lawdy," where an Anglo might recall in his mind the words of a white spiritual gone Afro, or tone the misery of a deep down blues. Thus to ease work, whites and blacks mingled their spirituals and blues, their ballads and chants into common sounds, common burdens. Entwined were images from work—one-horse plow, goose-necked hoe, cotton sack with a strop over the shoulder—symbols that would fade only when the culture was gone.

I was born just at the time that the one-horse plow and planting seed by hand were giving way to two-mule, two-wheel cultivators and automatic planters. My life in the early years was at the heart of the reality and the myth. When I was old enough to drag a flour sack down the row I picked and felt the softness clinging to sweaty palms, and stopped at times to put my face in the sack to breathe the fragrance that belongs only to cotton. Feel and fragrance—and with them the sounds of songs black and white, more black than white, old or made up on the spot, filled with the hope that things would be better by and by, the dream repeated whether I worked in a Red River bottom or some black waxy prairie. Later as I looked back I realized that I had been part of and witness to the creation of the most imaginative, richest cultural phenomenon in Texas—the common-meter hymns of Europe reshaped into the blues with the syncopated drum beat of Africa.

From a later viewpoint I was more able to comprehend how historical event or political change worked for or against ethnic and cultural mixing, but not why prejudice, particularly ethnic, remains alive and destructive long after the fancied reason has been forgotten.

In the ten years that Texas was a republic colonists expressed feelings against Mexicans by the often sounded "Remember the Alamo! Remember Goliad!" and toward Indians not so much for depredations in Texas but for long remembered bloodshed in the "dark and bloody ground" that was Kentucky. The popular mood, stirred by raids near Austin and favored by President Mirabeau B. Lamar, was to subdue or remove Mexicans and Indians, a

task to be assigned to the Texas Rangers. Mexicans battled sporadically but yielded. In 1840, Comanches attempted negotiation with the Anglos but it ended in bloodshed on both sides and annihilation of the Comanches in the battle of Plum Creek. Peaceful mingling was no longer a possibility.

In the same ten years the question of annexation to the United States raised other ethnic and cultural problems more emotional, more irrational than those from Mexicans or Indians. Most Texans, who were Americans before they were Texans, were strongly in favor of annexation. Southern by birth or by conviction, they saw annexation as an opportunity for expansion of the slavery system as it was practiced in the South. Anglos and Afros had made a pragmatic adjustment to each other, predictably favoring Anglos.

Within the United States slavery was regarded by many as a serious obstacle to annexation. The abolitionist movement was rapidly gaining strength. To its leaders annexation of Texas could only be an expansion of slavery. After long and bitter negotiation the slavery question was settled in favor of Texas, a decision that irrevocably cast Texas with the South politically, and made war with Mexico inevitable. October 13, 1845, Texas was admitted to the Union as a slave state. February 19, 1846, the Stars and Stripes floated from the top of the mast; the Lone Star flag, in the hearts and minds of Texans, remained the uniting symbol of the Texas myth.

True to their threat, Mexican soldiers crossed the Rio Grande and April 25, 1846, shed Anglo blood on Texas soil. Expansionists in the United States saw an opportunity to push what had come to be called "Manifest Destiny": "The fulfillment of our manifest destiny to overspread the continent allotted by Providence for the free development of our yearly multiplying millions." God gave the sanction; Mexicans the excuse. After two years of fighting the Mexicans yielded and signed the Treaty of Guadalupe Hidalgo, a treaty in which Mexico relinquished all claims to Texas above the Rio Grande and for fifteen million dollars ceded New Mexico and California to the United States. Manifest destiny had been achieved. The United States extended from the Atlantic to the Pacific, and out of the new territory carved parts of New Mexico, Oklahoma, Kansas, Wyoming, and Colorado, all of which had been a part of Texas.

Texas as a state prospered. The population, now including early French and German settlers, had increased to approximately 600,000. New and old settlers moved a hundred miles west into what had been Indian territory. Culture of the South began to be mingled with the newer culture of the West.

At the end of the Mexican War four major cultures survived in Texas: Indian, Anglo, Afro, and Mexican. The Indians had to go; so did their culture. In 1855, in a consensus that the only way to control Indians was to isolate them on reservations, a method used in older states, the surviving Indians were moved to a 12,000-acre tract along the Brazos. Ethnic or cultural mingling was precluded and tensions fostered. In 1859, because of complaints from settlers, the Indians were forced to resettle in Indian territory. Mexicans on newly occupied Anglo territory were not forced onto reservations but they were driven to resettle among their own kind. Some found places in what became the "Little Mexico" of San Antonio; others built their *jacales* nearer the Rio Grande, where for the most part they were ignored. Mexicans, unable to forget their defeat in war or the appropriation of their land, distilled their hatred of the Anglos, the people they called *gringos* or *los diablos Tejanos*. Anglos responded with spic or Mex. I regret the years they were adversaries. Living as I did in northeast Texas, I was in college before I saw a Mexican, heard a Spanish word except *tamale*, tapped my foot to the rhythm of a *mariachi* band.

Anglo and Afro remained master and slave, but abolitionists were gaining ground north of the Mason-Dixon Line and the passion for freedom on one side, the struggle to maintain the status quo on the other, led to breaking down the usually unspoken adjustment between master and slave and multiplying causes of friction between them. Their slave economy and customs of life threatened from the north, southern slaveholders and pro-slavery Texans began to talk of secession as preferable to what they considered Yankee outrage. In the heat on both sides events moved rapidly toward war. November 6, 1860, Abraham Lincoln was elected president of the United States on an anti-slavery ticket. December 24, 1860, South Carolina seceded from the Union. March 2, 1861, exactly a quarter of a century after the declaration of independence from Mexico, Texas declared independence from the United States. The sound of cannon at Fort Sumter shook Texas as it did the whole of the South.

To the Feds it was a war of rebellion, to the Rebs a war for southern independence, to less committed Texans it remained "The Late Unpleasantness." To

images

soldiers and civilians, Yankees and Rebels alike, images of camp and battlefield and young men dying, images preserved as tintypes, became part of the record of war. Stories abounded of a soldier whose life was saved when a bullet was stopped by a New Testament or a tintype of a loved one in his breast pocket. Photographs of Confederate soldiers posed or in action survived: There was little action on Texas soil to be photographed.

There are, however, written records of sentiment and experience. October 1, 1861, William Cleaver, first cousin to Missouri Ann, a young enlistee in Sibley's Brigade, wrote his wife: "I . . . being about to submit my mortal body to the uncertainties of the present war waged against the Confederate States of America under the auspices of the usurper and despot Abraham Lincoln. . . ." July 1, 1862, he was killed by Mexican Union soldiers in ambush while crossing the Rio Grande in the Mesilla Valley, New Mexico. For four years letters and diaries came back with their burden of battle and epidemic and death and despair—despair in the knowledge that, though the war was won, the South they cherished would be lost.

The surrender at Appomattox came April 9, 1865, but news was slow in reaching Texas. May 13, five weeks after the surrender, Colonel Rip Ford attacked three hundred Union soldiers at Palmito Ranch near Brownsville. With Rebel yells and artillery fire he killed thirty and captured one hundred and thirteen. From his prisoners he learned that the war was over. Texans could brag that, though they had lost the war, they had won the last battle.

Defeated, burdened in heart and mind, furloughed at last, Confederate soldiers rode their horses home if they had them, walked if they didn't. The Texas they returned to was not the Texas they had left. Their cultural identity had been fragmented. The Emancipation Proclamation, signed January 1, 1863, celebrated June 19, the date the slaves in Texas knew they were free, ended the black-white relationship that had existed since 1619. Their relationship was no longer master and slave. It was boss and hired hand, or landowner and tenant farmer. The Union promise of forty acres and a mule was never realized. The argument whether emancipation had made life better for the ex-slaves was a part of my growing-up experience. Slaves who had belonged to the Witherspoons and their neighbors moved out of slave cabins and built the same kind of cabins a mile or so away. In a cabin or two, or working beside an ex-slave or two, even in hard times, they argued that it was better to be free than to have a good *massa*. In contrast, among the Anglos, Yankees and the war were the evil of their lives. My grandmother blamed our hard times on "that old war."

In the two decades before and during the war immigrants from Europe—Germans, French, Czechs, Swedes, and others—settled in Texas to escape the political and economic oppression in their homelands, the Germans and Czechs in such numbers that before the end of the century Anglos called their strips of settlement the German belt and the Czech belt. Age-old hatreds imported from Europe by some ethnic groups were kept alive in Texas. Anglos, worried about what was happening to their identity and to their ownership of land, found reasons to resent the strangers. Some immigrants, so recently arrived that they could not be real Texans, had been too outspoken against the war; others had refused to serve. Distrust between Anglos and Germans intensified until in 1875 the violence called the Mason County War broke out. Threats were exchanged. A German settler was shot down on the street. As danger increased, it was necessary for the Texas Rangers to enter in and maintain peace. World War I aroused old fears that Germans were more loyal to Kaiser Wilhelm than they were to the United States. Rumors went the rounds. German classes in schools were forbidden. In World War II as a counterintelligence agent in the army I discovered how near the surface were the old enmities, old distrust. How often I had to scotch rumors about third-generation Germans accused of having a swastika in the house and teaching their children to say "Heil Hitler."

Sensible Anglos discounted rumors as rumors and accepted that these European immigrants had brought new ethnic blood, new ethnic culture, new interests in agriculture. In towns like Castroville, New Braunfels, and Fredericksburg they built houses and barns that looked more European than southern. They brought new sounds of music, of language, of laughing and dancing strange to people who had been brought up in the severity of frontier life.

Among other changes there was a perceptible movement toward urbanization, chiefly toward San Antonio, Houston, Dallas, Austin, and the community that was to be Fort Worth, each of a distinctive character, each as much a creation of location, economy, government as any New England town. As early as 1718 San Antonio was ethnically and culturally a Spanish-Mexican town, in its Indian population a challenge to mission-building Spanish *padres*. Houston, founded in 1837 on Buffalo Bayou, served as capital of Texas until Austin became the government town. Houston, with access to land and sea, became a railroad center through which thousands of bales of cotton were trans-shipped each year, chiefly to destinations in Europe. In 1841 John Neely Bryan built a log cabin on the Trinity River at the crossing of the First National Road. His cabin has survived. A central market for cotton, Dallas grew.

By 1846 settlers had moved west of Austin and San Antonio and the present Fort Worth and Waco—a move that was cultural as well as physical. The southern culture concentrated in east Texas was diluted in the mingling with the developing ranch culture of the West. Before the Civil War cattle ranching had shifted from east to southwest Texas, and to a mingling of Anglos and Mexicans. In that area aptly called the brush country the myth of the cowboy, whether Anglo or Mexican *vaquero*, had its beginning, a myth in which the two rode together, sharing language, lore, and custom. Words like *lariat*, *rodeo*, and *ranchero* crept into English usage.

The war over, the Indians gone, the buffaloes gone—cattlemen looking farther west saw the great plains with free rangeland stretching farther than the eye could see, an empire waiting to be exploited. By 1870 cattle-raising had become an industry with thousands of marketable beasts grazing the range, identifiable to the owner only by his registered brand. Before the war, cattle trails had led to Louisiana and California. After the war, major markets shifted to the north and east, with the nearest shipping points at Abilene and Dodge City, Kansas. Enterprising cattlemen pointed their drives north over newly beat-out trails, the Chisholm Trail to become a legend in song and story. The trails a thousand to fifteen hundred miles of open plains, cowboys alone in the saddle, or on guard around the chuck wagon at night, passed their time putting in song and story nostalgically, dramatically cowboy life from roundup to stampede to the end of the trail. With the help of journalists who may or may not have been on the range the romance grew in imagination with a sentiment that survived after reality intervened. Fort Worth, incorporated in 1873, reached by a railroad in 1876, replaced Abilene and Dodge City as shipping points, and cattle trains replaced cattle trails. Fort Worth emerged as the capital of the cattle empire and the cultural gateway to the West. The last drive from southwest Texas took place in 1885.

But the image of the cowboy on his bronco, in his hat and chaps and spurs to boot, the lonely figure on the lonely prairie, had entered the American imagination too deeply to be erased. Long after farmers had broken up the range with barbed-wire fences the cowboy remained a popular subject for ballad-maker, painter, sculptor, and photographer. Hundreds of miles away from the cattle country photographers in their studies furnished cowboy or cowgirl hat, bandana, and fake six-shooter in fake holster for anyone who fancied himself in appearance if not in character a rider of the range.

Enterprising photographers added other props—flowing shawl, coonskin cap, long rifle, dandy's hat and coat, ornate chair—anything to give the subject a different image of himself. With their improvement and skill, photographers no longer had to insist on a pose so rigid that the image came out flat, stare-eyed. When camera and tripod became portable, photographers traveled country roads, where people were eager for pictures of themselves in their best clothes, the backdrop their house, the props a favorite dog or horse. By 1890 people in town and country used photographs as well as the family Bible to record and perpetuate their history. One such photograph has been in my mind for more than fifty years. A young woman was killed in an accident. Her stricken family was more stricken because they had no photograph to remember her by. When she was in her coffin a photographer came and took a picture of her with grieving relatives standing by. Her mother put the picture in the family album beside the family Bible.

The camera reflects the image before it, but not always satisfactorily to viewers concerned—the light of life escapes it. A mirror image would not seem so. Amateur criticism was openly voiced. In spite of the fidelity of the photograph, viewers disagreed vocally: "Hit's a spittin' likeness of you-all if I ever seen one," or from another, "I cain't see no favor in it a-tall." No matter the appearance—bug-eyed, slack-jawed, or regular-featured—it was a fixed image, a confrontation that a subject could ponder and learn something about himself or someone else.

In 1888 George Eastman invented the roll film and put it on the market. No longer dependent on the studio or the itinerant photographer, picture-taking, less expensive, less demanding in skill, was shifted to the home, the school, the picnic. Taking

pictures of each other became a pastime. The poses less formal, the images more candid, people could look at themselves and each other with sharper perception of ways to dress, better postures, more favorable seemings. Acceptable pictures were sent off to be enlarged and framed for hanging on the wall. The more family effigies hanging in the front room, the higher the social position of the family. The camera had become an almost universal instrument of societal change. Talking about the faces in the pictures was entertainment on a dull Sunday evening. From my youth I recall a too critical response to the man of the house who ended his talk about the woman hanging over the fireplace with, "She was a good woman." A man who had dropped in squinted at the picture and said, "She might a-been a good woman but she was God-awful ugly."

January 10, 1901, the Lucas Gusher at Spindletop shot drilling pipe through the top of the derrick, spread crude oil over the area, and became forerunner of far-reaching economic, political, and cultural change. People rushed to see the wall. F. J. Trost rushed from his studio in Port Arthur and made the photograph that for many is the symbol of Texas oil.

Fifty years later I was appointed director of the Oral History of Texas Oil Pioneers, a project directed at taped interviews with men and women who could record authentic history of how people lived and worked in the early fields and the changes they had witnessed through the years. From having lived in Port Arthur in 1933, I had many impressions of the impact of oil on a refinery town and the kinds of people who could add their experiences to the history.

For six years intermittently I worked at Spindletop, Sour Lake, Batson, and Saratoga, interviewing any old-timer who would be interviewed. I spent days with Al and Curt Hamill, brothers, the only survivors of the crew that drilled the Lucas Gusher. Theirs was a story of hard work, ingenuity in improvising as they worked, the dramatic moment when the pipes began rising, the oil spraying like rain, an equally dramatic moment when the first Texas oil fire burst into flame.

I interviewed more than a hundred others—lawyers, doctors, lease hounds, wigglestick men, boll weevils, roughnecks, roustabouts, wildcatters, women who helped the men. Experiences from all these created in my mind a sense of time and place and people drawn from around the world by the magic of what they called black gold. I had secondhand images of oil fields with derricks crowding derricks, of men at work, of men and mules struck dead by odorless gas. Many of the images were those created by photographers who risked ever-present danger to capture the drama the world had not seen before. In less dramatic scenes they showed derrick men building derricks higher and higher, tong gangs laying pipelines to carry away oil from overflowing wells, carpenters building houses for workers and their families in the shadow and danger of derricks.

Oil and people. Together they made changes in the images of Texas as a cotton and cattle state. Workers with their families arrived from the oil fields of Pennsylvania and West Virginia. Cotton field workers, their crops destroyed by pink bollworms, got to Spindletop any way they could, drawn by the promise of three dollars a day, twelve hours on, twelve off. City people, American and European, with a newspaper picture of a gusher in hand, bought tickets or rode the rods. A new and intriguing culture was in the making. People made it and kept it in memory. In the middle or on the fringe of an oil field, photographers left a graphic history of how and where the people lived.

At Spindletop in 1902, before conservation, production unregulated, oil flowed in such quantity that the price dropped to three cents a barrel, while drinking water rose to a nickel a glass. Yet oil braced the economy through World War I and into the national slump. In 1932, under weakly enforced conservation and the impact of the east Texas field, gasoline sold at the pump for ten cents a gallon. Thus the Texas economy with all its social and cultural implications went from boom to bust—to what was soon called the Great Depression. Photographers faced a new challenge. They needed work; the government created work for them—that of making in one exposure when they could an artistic expression and a comment on the human condition—the same to serve as historical record and weapon for the social reformer. Such was the work of photographers employed by the Works Progress Administration, as I witnessed on an occasion in the Big Thicket. The photographer was snapping pictures of an unusual log house—unusual because of an eave extended over the stick-and-dirt chimney to protect it from rain. When he had finished, a daughter of the family asked if he would take a picture of her. He was willing but there was a problem. She had no shoes to wear and it wasn't fittin' for a girl her age to have her picture made barefooted. She stared at my crepe-soled loaf-

images

ers and asked if she could borrow them to have her picture made. I took them off. She put them on. The picture was made. I got my shoes back. He got a picture. So did she.

Though our working time together was less than a day, I knew what had been asked of him: the definition in image of abstract words such as misery, despair, loneliness—images that beget compassion. As I went my way, I knew that there to be recorded were the faces, the eyes of people waiting in soup lines, men selling apples on street corners, families in rattletrap cars on the way out to California, women in rags, children with hunger in their faces waiting at the door which to them seemed a heartless relief agency. Misery no longer needed to be defined. It was manifested in faces in city slums, on sharecropper farms, in hobo camps, until compassion demanded government rescue, whether of individual or community, whether from disasters brought on by panic, pestilence, storm, or flood. No doubt, as documentary, a picture is worth a thousand words.

In the four years before Pearl Harbor I took my recording machine and traveled all of Texas—surveying life on broad highways and back country roads, main streets and back streets—following my own plan to record in story and song anything I found that was representative of an ethnic group, an ethnic culture. My findings were of infinite variety and richness as I went to Negro Baptist churches, Czech *sokols*, Cajun French *fais-do-dos*, or any other gathering place. At times I found overlappings that seemed to intimate amalgamation; at others I found ethnic groups holding onto their language in the knowledge that to lose the language was to lose the culture; at others I found ethnic groups bound together for no purpose but political pressure. At no time did I find a community that in its mixture and togetherness would make valid de Crèvecoeur's melting pot theory. Too often I saw that misunderstanding, as in "The Ballad of Gregorio Cortez," leads to prejudice, prejudice to hatred, hatred to violence, violence to death.

December 21, 1968, in a dawn of heightened colors, I stood in the spectator's stand at Cape Canaveral among people heightened in spirit by awe and expectation. On a launching pad in front of us, a mile away, Apollo 8 stood in majestic splendor, awaiting the blast-off that would send it in orbit around the moon. Suddenly there was a piercing roar, and a cloud of smoke and steam orange-red in flame covered the lower part of the gantry. Impact from the blast struck. My sleeves and pants legs fluttered and tugged, and left me feeling unstable. Then the cone was lifted into light, gold at the tip, silver on the rounded sides. There was a moment of untempered applause and then silence in awareness of the sweep of history.

Out of awesome space a voice came back to the world, a human voice saying, "In the beginning God created the heaven and the earth." And the anticipated "So God created man in his *own* image, in the image of God created he him; male and female created he them." Not a word about color of skin, kinky hair, slanted eyes. Just male and female.

Another frontier crossed. When I think of it I think of Jane Witherspoon and Missouri Ann Cleaver, two women who crossed a frontier as awesome, and of the multitudes who crossed before and after them. I think of the Institute of Texan Cultures, where thousands of people meet to show their ethnic costumes, speak their own languages, sing their songs, dance their dances—all in a spirit of tolerance that pressages hope and expectation for all mankind.

The alternative? A photograph sent from outer space by Apollo 7 defines the narrowness of the Texas coast, how little space. It is not the thread of ethnicity but the thread of humanity that draws us all together.

William A. Owens

A photographic portrait

pre-1869

pre-1869

James Buckner "Buck" Barry. *E. Drane* (active ca. 1853).
Daguerreotype. Corsicana, Navarro County, June 1853. Collection of Lawrence T. Jones.

Barry (1821–1906) was a frontiersman, a Texas Ranger, a cattle rancher, an Indian fighter, and a state legislator. He was the first sheriff of Navarro County, which as part of the frontier, covered all territory between the Brazos and Trinity rivers west to the New Mexico territory. His memoirs are considered among the best recollections of day-to-day settler life on the Texas frontier. This daguerreotype is possibly the oldest surviving photograph made in Texas.

"Harriet Durst [Hopkins] and her daughter."
Unidentified photographer.
Ambrotype. Possibly Leon County, late 1850s or early 1860s. Barker Texas History Center, the University of Texas at Austin.

Harriet Matilda Durst was the daughter of two early Texas settlers.

Mary Ann Adams Maverick and two other women. *Unidentified photographer.*

Tintype. Possibly San Antonio, Bexar County, 1856 or after. Barker Texas History Center, University of Texas at Austin.

When Maverick (1818–1898) came to Texas in 1838 with her new husband, Samuel Augustus Maverick, she began keeping a diary later published as the *Memoirs of Mary A. Maverick.* In the book, this photograph appears with the caption under the year 1849: "November 5th, Mrs. Elliott, Susan Hays and I had our daguerreotypes taken at Whitfield's gallery. . . ." It is possible that this tintype is a copy of the original daguerreotype made in 1849. However, if this is not a copy, it could not have been made before 1856, when the tintype process was invented.

Pliny Rutherford Fleming, Jr. Possibly *Pierce and Brother* (active ca. 1853).

Daguerreotype. Green Lake, Calhoun County, 1853. Institute of Texan Cultures.

Sam Houston. *Unidentified photographer.* Daguerreotype. Possibly Austin, Travis County, about 1850. Texas State Library.

This image of Sam Houston (1793–1863) is one of the best known photographs of the first president of the Republic of Texas. Although the image could have been made as early as the beginning of the 1840s, Houston's appearance dates the image around 1850, when he was serving in the United States legislature as a senator.

Mirabeau Buonaparte Lamar. *Unidentified photographer.* Daguerreotype. Possibly Austin, Travis County, 1850s. San Jacinto Museum of History Association.

Lamar (1798–1859), a commander in the revolutionary army of the Republic of Texas, later served as the second president of the Republic. Although he is remembered favorably for his education programs, he is also known for his policy of eliminating all Indians from Texas.

Thomas F. McKinney. *Unidentified photographer.*
From a copy print of a daguerreotype. Austin, Travis County, mid-1850s. Texas State Library.
McKinney (1801–1873) was an early financier of the revolution and the Republic. In the 1850s, when this photograph was likely made, McKinney resided in Travis County near Austin, where he raised pedigree horses.

Burros with a load of corn. Possibly *William DeRyee* (active 1858–1861).

Albumen print, varnished. San Antonio, Bexar County, about 1860. Library of the Daughters of the Republic of Texas.

Woman in striped blouse. *Unidentified photographer.*
Ambrotype. Tyler, Smith County, mid-1860s. Smith County Historical Society Archives.

John Wheeler Bunton. *Unidentified photographer.*
Ambrotype. Possibly Hays or Caldwell County, early 1860s. Barker Texas History Center, University of Texas at Austin.

Bunton (1807–1879) was a signer of the Texas Declaration of Independence and represented Mina (later known as Bastrop) at the convention of 1836, where he helped to draft the constitution of the Republic.

Surrender of the federal troops to the forces of Ben McCulloch at the beginning of the Civil War. *Unidentified photographer.*

Ambrotype. San Antonio, Bexar County, about 1861. Texas State Library.

The buildings identify this scene as the view facing north on Soledad Street in San Antonio. This photograph is believed to show the willing surrender of Brigadier General David Emanuel Twiggs to the Confederate forces.

The store of Arthur H. Edey & Kirsten. Possibly *Louis de Planque* (1842–1898).

Albumen carte-de-visite. Corpus Christi, Nueces County, between 1865 and 1870. La Retama Public Library.

The animal figures were used to identify different warehouses so that illiterate customers could be directed to the correct store.

Two soldiers in a Confederate camp. *Unidentified photographer.* Ambrotype. Houston vicinity, Harris County, 1861. Collection of Lawrence T. Jones.

These soldiers are probably members of the Milam County Greys, who were mustered into service in 1861 and became Company G of the 5th Texas Volunteer Infantry Regiment, Hood's Texas Brigade.

Emzy Taylor and G. M. Taylor. *Unidentified photographer.* Tintype. McLennan County, 1861. Collection of Lawrence T. Jones.

These brothers were members of Company E of the 4th Texas Volunteer Infantry Regiment, Hood's Texas Brigade, also known as the Lone Star Guards.

Tintypes were especially popular during the Civil War, because the metal pictures could be sent through the mail without breaking. Many soldiers had their portraits made to send to loved ones as momentos.

pre-1869

Street scene. *R. C. Morris* (active 1850s).
From a copy print. Houston, Harris County, 1856. Collection of Colleen Talmadge Claybourn.
This photograph is thought to be the oldest surviving image of Houston.

New Braunfels dwelling. *Henry Doerr* (b. 1826, active 1877–1905).
Albumen carte-de-visite. New Braunfels, Comal County, late 1860s.
Library of Congress.
New Braunfels was founded May 21, 1845, by Prince Carl Solms-Braunfels, stepson of the King of Hanover; it was the first German settlement in Texas arranged by a German colonization company.

Studio portrait of a woman. *Unidentified photographer.*
Ambrotype. Possibly Austin vicinity, Travis County, late 1850s.
Collection of Lawrence T. Jones.

Studio portrait of a woman. *Unidentified photographer.*
Ambrotype, hand tinted. Possibly Austin vicinity, Travis County,
late 1850s. Collection of Darnelle Vanghel.

1870's

1870's

A Freemason. *George Schuwirth* (d. 1906, active 1877–1905).

Albumen carte-de-visite. Austin, Travis County 1875–1881. Barker Texas History Center, University of Texas at Austin.

The first organization of black Masons in Texas was in San Antonio in 1871. By the 1880s, a number of different secret fraternities served some of the social needs of the black community and provided insurance and capital for business ventures.

James Stephen Hogg at his newspaper. *Unidentified photographer.*

From a copy print of an ambrotype. Longview, Gregg County, between 1871 and 1873. San Jacinto Museum of History Association.

Before serving as governor of the state, James Hogg (1851–1906) ran newspapers in Longview and Quitman. His reformist editorial policies were early expressions of the directions his administration would take.

"Wild Tom and Buffalo Bill, the Texian scouts." *McArthur Cullen Ragsdale* (1849–1944).

Albumen carte-de-visite. Central Texas, possibly near New Braunfels, Comal County, between 1870 and 1875. Sophienberg Memorial Association Archives.

This is certainly not William F. Cody, the famous "Buffalo Bill." This man may have used the same nickname, or it may be that he and his friend adopted western names and western clothes just for this picture.

"Lucy, who belonged to A. C. Harris." *Barr and Wright* (firm active 1870–1879).

Tintype in paper protector. Houston, Harris County, about 1870. San Jacinto Museum of History Association.

"Senatorial Group of the 15th Legislature."
Hamilton Briscoe Hillyer (1835–1903).
Composite of albumen prints. Austin, Travis County,
1876. Fayette Heritage Museum/Archives.

William Ralph Haynes. *Unidentified photographer.*
Tintype. Austin or Burnet, Travis or Burnet County, about 1873. Collection of Lawrence T. Jones.

Robert Jenkins Onderdonk. *Doerr and Jacobson* (firm active 1876–1879).
Tinted albumen carte-de-visite. San Antonio, Bexar County, 1879. Collection of Lawrence T. Jones.
Onderdonk moved to San Antonio in 1878 or 1879 and became an influential Texas painter. Several of his children also became noted Texas artists.

1870's

Cathedral Hall on Broadway. *Louis de Planque* (1842–1898). Albumen carte-de-visite. Corpus Christi, Nueces County, probably after 1878. La Retama Public Library.

A Mexican *jacal*. *Unidentified photographer*. Albumen boudoir print. San Antonio, Bexar County, between 1878 and 1880. San Antonio Museum Association.

A *jacal* was a common type of frontier housing with a thatched roof and walls made of woven sticks and brush. *Jacales* remained in use into the twentieth century.

Madame Lola Windsor and Professor William Windsor, LLB, phrenologists, in front of their lecture hall. *Unidentified photographer.*
Albumen print. Gatesville, Coryell County, about 1875. Texas Collection, Baylor University.

Office of the Waco *Examiner. Unidentified photographer.*
Albumen cabinet print. Waco, McLennan County, after 1873. Texas Collection, Baylor University.

The *Examiner* was established in 1867. By 1873 the paper was publishing both weekly and daily editions, which are advertised in the photograph.

1870's

Townscape. *McArthur Cullen Ragsdale*
(1849–1944).
Albumen carte-de-visite. Unidentified location,
central Texas, probably before 1875.
Fort Concho Museum.

Ragsdale was an itinerant photographer who traveled through central Texas before settling at Fort Concho in 1875. This is probably one of the many small Texas towns that Ragsdale visited as he made his living by setting up shop temporarily in one place after another.

"Beauties of the San Antonio River." *Henry L. Bingham* (active 1877–1879).

Albumen stereograph. San Antonio, Bexar County, June 1879. Amon Carter Museum.

1870's

"Pagrias." *Doerr and Jacobson* (firm active 1876–1879).
Albumen stereograph print. San Antonio, Bexar County, late 1870s. Amon Carter Museum.
The women who sold songbirds were popular subjects for photographers and other artists.

East side of De Leon Plaza.
Unidentified photographer.
From a copy negative.
Victoria, Victoria County, late 1870s. Institute of Texan Cultures.

This view is taken looking south on Main Street, toward Constitution. The public scales for weighing wagons with their loads are on the center right.

An early Austin musical ensemble. *Unidentified photographer.* Albumen print. Austin, Travis County, 1877 or 1878. Austin History Center.

McArthur Cullen Ragsdale's traveling photographic tent studio. *McArthur Cullen Ragsdale* (1849–1944).
Albumen carte-de-visite. Possibly central Texas, about 1870. Fort Concho Museum.

1880's

The burning of the Colonial Capitol. *Samuel B. Hill* (1841?–1917).

Albumen stereograph. Austin, Travis County, November 9, 1881. Collection of Lawrence T. Jones.

The second capitol in Austin, known as both the Colonial Capitol and the Old Stone Capitol, was constructed in 1853 and destroyed by fire in 1881. Hill photographed several views of the burning building, which was in sight of his studio on Congress Avenue. Having gained a reputation with these photographs, Hill later used a line drawing of the burning capitol as his logo.

Interior of the Colonial Capitol after the fire. *Hamilton Briscoe Hillyer* (1835–1903). Albumen stereograph. Austin, Travis County, November 1881. Collection of Lawrence T. Jones.

The Brigham–San Jacinto Monument, as seen at the unveiling at the Galveston Pavillion. *Phillip H. Rose* (b.1829?, active 1880–1887).
Albumen cabinet print. Galveston, Galveston County, 1881.
Fort Bend County Museum.

This monument was designed as a grave marker for Benjamin Rice Brigham, who fell at the Battle of San Jacinto in 1836.

Interior of Frances Newberry and J. M. Holbrook's home after their wedding. *Francis Parker* (active 1882–1908).
Albumen print. El Paso, El Paso County, 1885. El Paso Public Library.

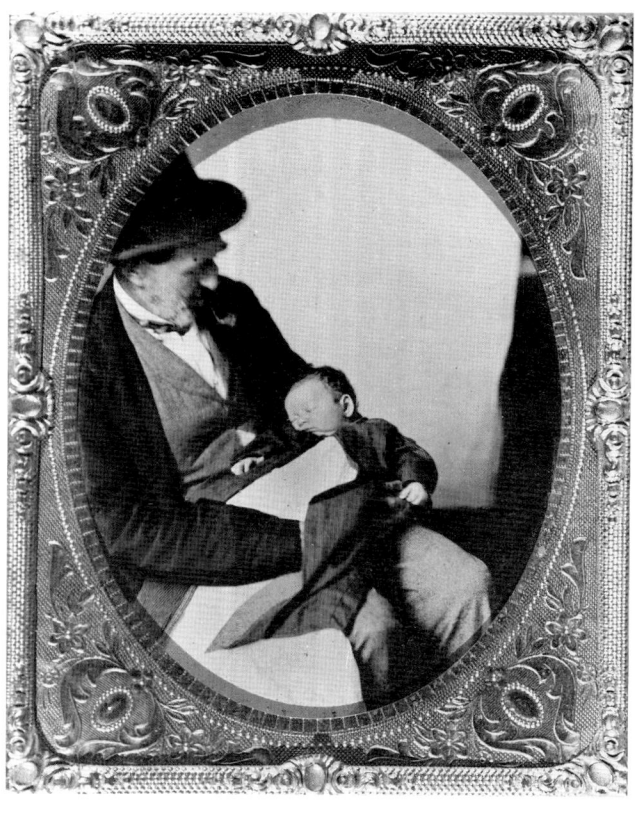

"J. W. Miles and Sullivan Miles." *Unidentified photographer.* Tintype. Brenham, Washington County vicinity, mid-1880s. Star of the Republic Museum.

Waldine and Erma Tauch. *Henry Tauch* (active 1884–1896). Albumen cabinet print. Fayetteville, Fayette County, about 1884. Fayette Heritage Museum/Archives. These are two daughters of the photographer.

A reunion of Texas veterans. *F. P. Cooper* (active 1882–1884).

Albumen print. Belton, Bell County, April 21, 1883. Texas Collection, Baylor University.

Such reunions of Texas veterans were annual affairs.

San Fernando de Bexar Cathedral. *Nicholas C. Winther* (active 1868–1885).

Albumen stereograph. San Antonio, Bexar County, early 1880s. San Antonio Museum Association.

The cornerstone of the original church structure was laid May 13, 1734. Later, the building was expanded, and the cornerstone of the new structure was laid September 27, 1868. The second tower was not completed until about 1900.

"Fort Davis at the height of development." *Unidentified photographer.*

"Enlisted men of Troop C, 3rd U.S. Cavalry." *Unidentified photographer.*

Modern gelatin silver prints from the original glass negatives. Fort Davis, Jeff Davis County, 1886–1889. Fort Davis National Historic Site.

The non-commissioned officers are, left to right: Sergeant John Wylie, Company I, 5th Infantry; Corporal Robert Dickson, Company I, 5th Infantry; Hospital Steward Jacob H. Appel; First Sergeant McHale; Quartermaster Sergeant Gustave Fahlbush; an unidentified first sergeant; and Commissary Sergeant Thomas H. Forsyth.

"Enlisted men of the 16th Infantry, posing behind post hospital." *Unidentified photographer.*

"Non-commissioned officers of Fort Davis posing behind post hospital."
Unidentified photographer.

Henrich Ludwig's "Phoenix" beer garden.
Unidentified photographer.
Gelatin silver print. New Braunfels, Comal County, about 1885. Sophienberg Memorial Association Archives.

"View on Bee Creek, two-and-one-half miles above Austin. The road under the Cliff leading to the Spring." *William James Oliphant* (1845–1930). Albumen print. Austin, Travis County, 1880s. San Antonio Museum Association.

"Mexican Mellicocher dealer." *A. V. Latourette* (active 1880s).
Albumen stereograph. San Antonio, Bexar County, 1880s. Amon Carter Museum.
Food vendors such as this man played an important part in life on Military Plaza in San Antonio during the nineteenth century.

"Chili-con-carne." *Unidentified photographer.*
From a copy print. San Antonio, Bexar County, 1887–1889. Institute of Texan Cultures.
The buildings in the background were on the south side of Military Plaza. Because early San Antonio custom was to eat late, this vendor kept lanterns on his table so that he could sell his tacos late into the night.

Art class at St. Mary's College. *Unidentified photographer.*
Albumen print. San Antonio, Bexar County, 1880s. San Antonio Museum Association.

Theodore Gentilz (1819–1906), a noted Texas artist, began teaching at St. Mary's College during the Civil War and remained there until 1894. Among the first settlers of Castroville, he came to Texas from France, where he had been an honored student at the National School of Mathematics and Drawing in Paris.

Playing cards. *Unidentified photographer.*
Gelatin silver print. New Braunfels, Comal County, 1880s. Sophienberg Memorial Association Archives.

Mesquite Ridge, the King's Place, 490 Delgado Street. *Charles F. King* (active late 1880s).

Albumen print. San Antonio, Bexar County, 1889. San Antonio Museum Association.

Exercise class at St. Mary's College. *Unidentified photographer.*
Collodio-chloride print. San Antonio, Bexar County, late 1880s. San Antonio Museum Association.

The present St. Mary's University had its origins in this school.

"Boots made by Joseph Lucchese which won first prize in the San Antonio International Exposition." *C. H. Savage* (active 1881–1896).
Albumen cabinet print. San Antonio, Bexar County, 1889. San Antonio Museum Association.

Four styles of brooms made by the La Grange Broom Manufacturing Company. *Conrad Petersen* (active 1882–1896).
Collodio-chloride cabinet print. La Grange, Fayette County, late 1880s. San Antonio Museum Association.

1880's

Ship's captain at the wheel. *Phillip H. Rose* (b.1829?, active 1880–1887).
Gelatin silver stereograph. Galveston, Galveston County, early 1880s. Rosenberg Library.
After 1875, Galveston maintained exports of more than $10,000,000 each year. Most of the goods were cotton and grain.

The studio of George Schuwirth. *George Schuwirth* (d. 1906, active 1877–1905).
Albumen cabinet print. Austin, Travis County, about 1880. Collection of Lawrence T. Jones.

1890's

1890's

Studio portrait of an infant in a sea shell. *McArthur Cullen Ragsdale* (1849–1944). Albumen cabinet print. San Angelo, Tom Green County, early 1890s. Fort Concho Museum.

Studio portrait of a young girl. *Henry H. Morris* (1869–1956). Albumen cabinet print. Galveston, Galveston County, 1890s. Harris County Heritage Society.

Two children in a crescent moon. *Franz Carl Hoffmann* (1879–1929).

Collodio-chloride cabinet print. New Braunfels, Comal County, late 1890s. Sophienberg Memorial Association Archives.

The photographer's daughter has identified these children as Carroll Hoffmann and Minnie Deutsch.

1890's

"The house where we were born." *Unidentified photographer.*
Gelatin silver print. Waxahachie, Ellis County vicinity, 1890s.
Ellis County Museum.

Residence of W. H. Abrams. *Unidentified photographer.*
Gelatin silver print. Dallas, Dallas County, 1890s. Dallas Historical Society.
Called "The Shingles," this home was built in 1888 by Edwin P. Cowan and sold to Abrams in 1893 for $20,000. The structure was demolished in 1930.

"Bulls and Bears, the Galveston Cotton Exchange." *Henry H. Morris* (1869–1956).

Gelatin silver print. Galveston, Galveston County, 1899. Rosenberg Library.

The Cotton Exchange evolved out of the Cotton Factors' Association of Galveston and was established as a corporation by act of the state legislature in 1875. Its purpose was to establish equitable prices for cotton, determine uniform wages, maintain rules and regulations, develop standards of classification, and promote the interests of cotton trade.

Interior of Dickerson brothers' store. *Unidentified photographer*.

Gelatin silver print. Possibly Mobeetie, Wheeler County, early 1890s. Panhandle Plains Museum.

George Eastman began marketing the first true snapshot cameras in 1888. The photographs made by the first two models of Kodaks are distinguished by the round image.

Two churches with steeples.
Possibly *Mr. Wiedermeyer* (active 1890s).
Modern gelatin silver prints made from the original glass negatives. Clifton, Bosque County, 1890s. Amon Carter Museum.
The photographer may have been a minister at a church in Clifton, an old Norwegian community.

Two children in a garden. Possibly
Mr. Wiedermeyer (active 1890s).

1890's

Independence Tree of Texas. Possibly *J. W. Morris* or *F. E. Beach* (active 1890s–early 1900s).

Gelatin silver cabinet print. West Columbia, Brazoria County, 1897. University of Texas at Arlington.

It was from this tree in front of the first Texas capitol that Texas' Declaration of Independence was read. It is also said that Santa Anna was chained to the tree when a prisoner.

Group at the Brigham–San Jacinto Monument. *Henry Stanton* (active 1890s).

Collodio-chloride print. La Porte, Harris County, 1890s. San Jacinto Museum of History Association.

This is the same monument pictured on page 72 after it had been placed on the San Jacinto Battlegrounds, a popular picnic spot since the Texas revolution.

"An exhibition held under the auspices of the San Antonio Art League." *Unidentified photographer.*
Albumen print. San Antonio, Bexar County, about 1894. San Antonio Museum Association.

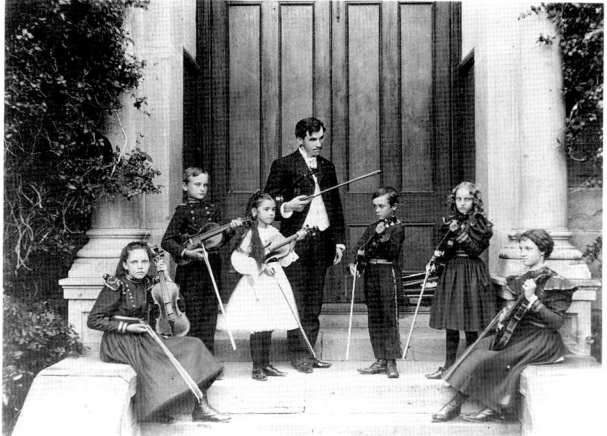

A violin class in front of an old schoolhouse. *Unidentified photographer.*
Gelatin silver print. San Angelo, Tom Green County, 1890s. Fort Concho Museum.

"Panorama of El Paso from the West." *Charles 3. Turrill* (1854–1927).

Six albumen prints. El Paso, El Paso County, 1891. Barker Texas History Center, the University of Texas at Austin.

The photographer moved the camera six times and made six separate negatives to create this panorama.

Grand Central Depot on Washington Street. *Unidentified photographer.* From a copy print. Houston, Harris County, 1894. Harris County Heritage Society.

Fiftieth anniversary of New Braunfels' founding. *H. Richter* (active 1890s).

Gelatin silver print. New Braunfels, Comal County, 1895. Sophienberg Memorial Association Archives.

1890's

The great Crush collision. *Jervis C. Deane* (b. 1860, active 1888–1900).

From a copy print. Crush, McLennan County, September 15, 1896. Texas Collection, Baylor University.

William George Crush, a ticket agent on the Katy Line, devised a promotional scheme attracting some 40,000 people to see two locomotives run together at a speed estimated at 90 miles per hour between Waco and West. Crush had been assured by mechanical engineers at the Katy roundhouses that the boilers would not burst on collision. However, two people lost their lives from the explosion and many others were injured, including the photographer, who lost an eye. Scott Joplin wrote "The Crush Collision March" to commemorate the event.

Flanagan's market. *Unidentified photographer.*
Collodio-chloride print. Midland, Midland County, 1895. Midland County Museum.
This photograph is an early example of a genre that developed over the next 40 years. Using a camera that made a 5 × 7 inch negative with a moderately wide-angle lens, the photographer posed a few people in the business where they worked. Itinerant photographers traveled from town to town making these business photographs, selling prints to the employees to make a living.

Horses and carts bearing cotton in Tyler Square. Possibly *C. A. Davis* (active late 1890s).
Gelatin silver print. Tyler, Smith County, about 1900. Smith County Historical Society Archives.

On the beach, Galveston. *Henry Stark* (active 1890s), from *Views in Texas*.
Gelatin silver print. Galveston, Galveston County, 1895–1896. Dallas Historical Society.
Stark was a photographer from Saint Louis who traveled in Texas during the winter of 1895–1896. He later made hand-bound books of his pictures.

"Group of San Angelo Wheelmen." *Unidentified photographer.*
Gelatin silver print. San Angelo, Tom Green County, 1897 or 1898.
Fort Concho Museum.

Farming in Marion County. *Henry Stark* (active 1890s), from *Views in Texas*. Gelatin silver print. Marion County, 1895–1896. Dallas Historical Society.

A farm in Fannin County, near Bonham. Henry Stark (active 1890s),
from *Views in Texas*.
Gelatin silver print. Bonham vicinity, Fannin County, 1895–1896. Encino Press.

"Parade around public square." [*Frank?*] *Hudson* (active 1893-1900). According to an article in the *Kansas City Star*, February 2, 1893, Henry Smith, a black man, was arrested by Henry Vance, the white sheriff, for public intoxication. Smith then declared revenge. When the body of Vance's daughter, Myrtle, was found in a field, Smith was accused of her rape and murder. A crowd of some 10,000 people from as far away as Little Rock and Wichita Falls gathered for the vigilante execution. "Governor Hogg telegraphed the officials [at Paris] to protect the negro from mob violence and after hearing of Smith's fate wired them to take the names of the parties principally concerned in the affair for prosecution, but it will never amount to anything."

"Little Myrtle Vance Avenged." *[Frank?] Hudson* (active 1893–1900).

"The Avengers of Little Myrtle Vance and the Villain brought to Justice." *[Frank?] Hudson* (active 1893–1900).

"Henry Vance and Family." *[Frank?] Hudson* (active 1893–1900).
Gelatin silver prints. Paris, Lamar County, February 1893. 110 and 112: Library of Congress. 111
and 113: Barker Texas History Center, University of Texas at Austin.

Portrait montage. *Samuel Anderson* (active 1884–1900) and unidentified photographers.

Gelatin silver and collodio-chloride prints and tintypes. Houston, Harris County, and southeast Texas, 1880s–1890s. Sam Houston Regional Library and Research Center.

1890's

Louise Recknagel on tricycle. *Friederike Recknagel* (1860–1956).
Modern gelatin silver print from the original glass negative. Round Top, Fayette County, about 1895. Collection of E. W Ahlrich.
Louise was the daughter of the photographer.

Pearl Baker wearing a dress decorated with photographs.
McArthur Cullen Ragsdale (1849–1944).
Albumen print (fragment). San Angelo, Tom Green County, about 1890. Fort Concho Museum.

Louis de Planque in costume for Columbus Day celebration.
Louis de Planque (1842–1898).
Gelatin silver cabinet card. Corpus Christi, Nueces County, early 1890s. La Retama Public Library.

"Where I learned the trade." Possibly *Joseph Edward Taulman* (1863–1946).
Gelatin silver print. Clifton, Bosque County, 1894. Barker Texas History Center, University of Texas at Austin.

1900's

1900's

"Brahma Bull belonging to the A. H. Pierce Estate." *Louis Melcher* (1870–1948).

Gelatin silver print. Pierce, Wharton County, early 1900s. Wharton County Museum.

One of the earliest Texas cattlemen was Abel Head "Shanghai" Pierce (1834–1900). Pierce began his ranching career in 1854 at Indianola on the ranch of Richard Grimes. Pierce began his own ranch in the early 1870s when he went into partnership with his brother, Jonathan Edwards Pierce. Pierce's ranch is responsible for introducing the base stock of Brahman cattle into Texas.

"Claude Jeffers (wearing vest) working with a bronc in a corral on the Matador Land and Cattle Company." *Erwin Evans Smith* (1886–1947).

Gelatin silver print. Possibly Motley County, 1908. Erwin E. Smith Collection, Library of Congress.

The Matador Ranch began with the partnership of A. M. Britton and H. H. Campbell in 1878. By 1910 the ranch covered more than one million acres.

Dormitory at Old Firehouse #5. *George Beach* (active 1901–1925). Gelatin silver print. Houston, Harris County, early 1900s. Harris County Heritage Society.

Checkout desk at the Carnegie Library. *Unidentified photographer.*

Gelatin silver print. Dallas, Dallas County, 1900s. Texas/Dallas History and Archives Division, Dallas Public Library.

Steel magnate and philanthropist Andrew Carnegie donated $41,000,000 to 1,500 cities to build 1,697 libraries between the years 1890 and 1917. Thirty Texas cities benefited; San Antonio, Dallas, and Houston received two grants each. The first Carnegie library in Dallas opened in 1901.

1900's

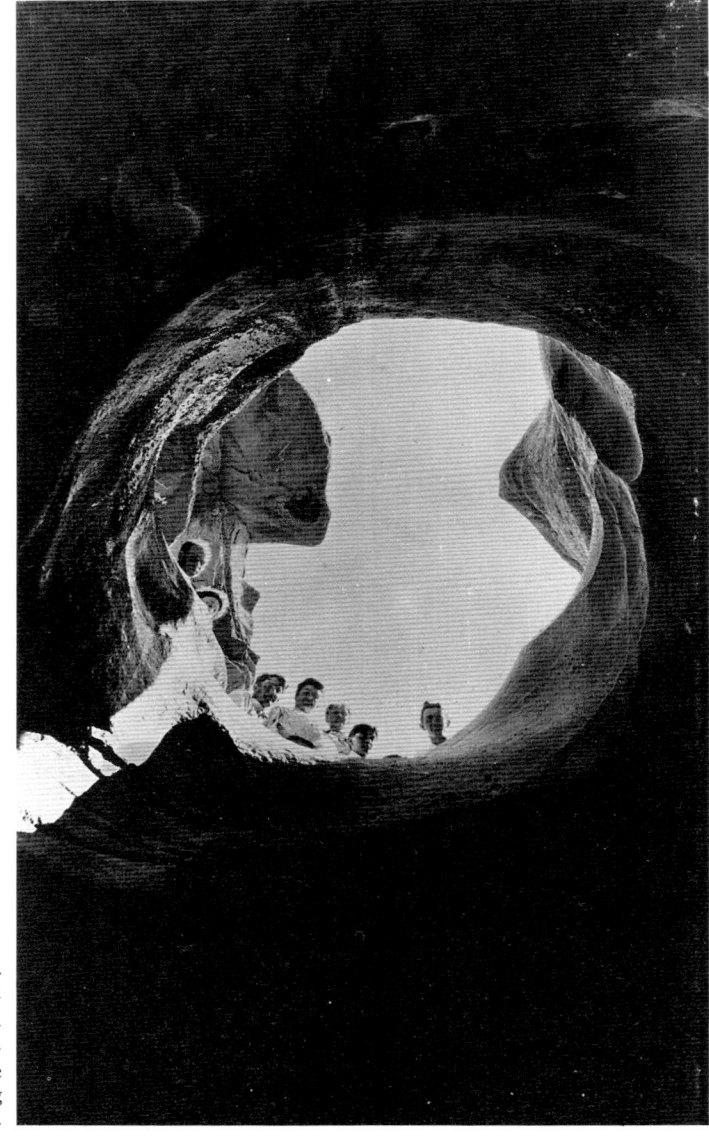

Looking down into Devil's Kitchen in Palo Duro Canyon.
Unidentified photographer.
Gelatin silver print. Randall County, about 1900.
Panhandle Plains Museum.
Palo Duro Canyon was the site of many picnics for the people of the Amarillo area, and it was an important part of the Goodnight-Loving trail, providing a natural pen from which cattle could not escape.

Family portrait at Silver Falls. *Erwin Evans Smith* (1886–1947).
Gelatin silver print. East of Crosbyton, Crosby County, late 1900s. Panhandle Plains Museum.
The Smith family—Mrs. H. C., George, Sallie, Henry, Viola, Eveline, Ruben, Barbara, and Frank—with Bert Batty and George Patullo. This is not the family of the photographer. Raised near Bonham, Erwin Smith wanted to be an artist. He left for art school in Boston with his photographic "sketches" of cowboys. There he met his partner, George Patullo, who was a writer for the *Boston Herald*. Smith and Patullo returned to Texas to photograph and write about cowboy life.

1900's

"Mexican home." *McArthur Cullen Ragsdale (1849–1944).*
Collodio-chloride print. San Angelo vicinity, Tom Green County, 1900s. Southwest Collection, Texas Tech University.
Much like the *jacal*, the dugout was a frontier style of home common on the plains.

E. W. Daniels' insurance office. *McArthur Cullen Ragsdale* (1849–1944).
Gelatin silver print. Possibly San Angelo, Tom Green County, about 1901.
Fort Concho Museum.

Cashier and auditing department, Edwin Chamberlain and Company. *Unidentified photographer*.

Gelatin silver print. San Antonio, Bexar County, 1900s. San Antonio Museum Association.

Left to right: Claude King, S. J. Bodger, F. Ramos, George Bodet, William Riddle, Jim Miller, and Edward King.

1900's

Buffalo drinking at a stream. *[Samuel?] Sherman* (active ca. 1896). Gelatin silver print. Amarillo vicinity, Potter County, 1900s. Panhandle Plains Museum.

Man with steer horns. *Unidentified photographer*. Gelatin silver postcard print. Mineola, Wood County, 1900s. Panhandle Plains Museum.

Elisabet Ney in her studio. *Ernst Raba* (1874–1951).

Gelatin silver print. Austin, Travis County, about 1900. San Antonio Museum Association.

Ney (1833–1907) was trained as a sculptor in her native Germany. She found little appreciation for her art in Texas when she arrived in 1870. Nearly twenty years later, however, she received a commission from the state to create statues of Sam Houston and Stephen F. Austin for the World's Fair of 1893. The original statues are now at the Elisabet Ney Studio in Austin; Italian marble facsimiles are in both the state and national capitols.

Four west Texas dandies making New Year's Day calls. *Unidentified photographer*.

Collodio-chloride print. San Angelo, Tom Green County, 1900s. Fort Concho Museum.

1900's

"Two men who formerly were slaves." *[Joseph?] Lux* (active late 1890s).
Gelatin silver print. Possibly Sealy, Austin County, about 1900. Barker Texas History Center, University of Texas at Austin.

Sallie Gertrude Goodman LeGrand with her head in the lap of Cely Lipscomb. *[Alonzo N.?] Callaway* (d. 1920, active 1878–1910).

Carbon print. Tyler, Smith County, June 1905. Smith County Historical Society Archives.

The daughter of Dr. William J. Goodman, Sallie was the belle of Tyler society. Her family home in Tyler is now the Goodman Museum.

Republican county convention. *Unidentified photographer.*

Gelatin silver print. La Grange, Fayette County, July 16, 1904. Fayette Heritage Museum/Archives.

Blacks traditionally belonged to the Republican party because Abraham Lincoln was a Republican. Because of the prejudice in the South, white Republicans fled to the Democratic party. Charles Gates, Convention Chairman, is seated in the judge's chair. Charles Toney, Secretary, is on the judge's stand. There were about 200 black delegates to this convention.

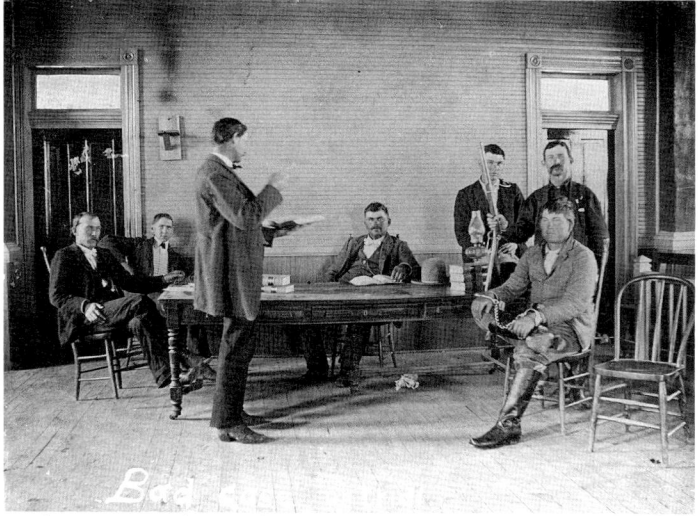

"Bad Case on Trial." *Unidentified photographer.*

Gelatin silver print. Dimmitt, Castro County, early 1900s. Panhandle Plains Museum.

A case held in the court of Lysius Gough. Bob Higgins, defendant, claimed that he had dug in the Palo Duro Canyon at a time when evidence showed that he was not there.

1900's

Train derailment. *Unidentified photographer.* Gelatin silver print. Possibly North Central Texas, 1900s. Texas/Dallas History and Archives Division, Dallas Public Library.

Locomotives at the Galveston wharves. *Verkin Studios* (active early 1900s).
Gelatin silver print. Galveston, Galveston County, 1907 or after. Rosenberg Library.

"Texas and Pacific Railroad 'Flier.'" *Benjamin West Kilburn* (1872–1909).
Gelatin silver stereograph. Dallas, Dallas County, 1909. Library of Congress.

Turntable at the Santa Fe yards. *Unidentified photographer.*
Gelatin silver print. Cleburne, Johnson County, about 1905. Layland Museum.
The Santa Fe shops were built at Cleburne in 1898 and are still operating there.

"Bodies among Ruins—Characteristic Scene in Galveston."
Unidentified photographer.
Gelatino-chloride stereograph. Galveston, Galveston County, 1900. Rosenberg Library.
On September 8, 1900, a hurricane hit Galveston Island. By evening winds were clocked at 120 miles per hour and five feet of water covered the city. Six thousand people were killed.

Ruins of a church after the Galveston flood.
Unidentified photographer.
Gelatin silver print. Galveston, Galveston County, September 1900. Rosenberg Library.

Camp Mabry Road, near Pease Park. *Dr. John Mathias Kuehne* (1872–1960).

Modern gelatin silver print from the original glass negative. Austin, Travis County, about 1901. Barker Texas History Center, University of Texas at Austin.

The Reverend George Mayfield Daniel and his son. *Unidentified photographer.*

Gelatin silver print. Atascosito vicinity, around 1908. Sam Houston Regional Library and Research Center.

The Reverend Daniel (1846–1918) arrived in Texas in 1867. He was a Baptist minister, ordained in 1873, and a peddler of religious tracts in east and southeast Texas. He lived in Willis from 1892 to 1907, and in Tyler from 1908 until his death. He was the grandfather of Price Daniel, governor of Texas from 1957 to 1963.

1900s

"Edwards County is famous for its mohair production." *Ichabel Nelson Hall* (active 1880s–1890s).

Gelatin silver print. Edwards County, 1903 or after. *Uvalde Leader-News*.

Woman training her dog to sit. *Unidentified photographer*.

Modern gelatin silver print from the original nitrate negative. Possibly Fort Worth, Tarrant County, about 1905. University of Texas at Arlington.

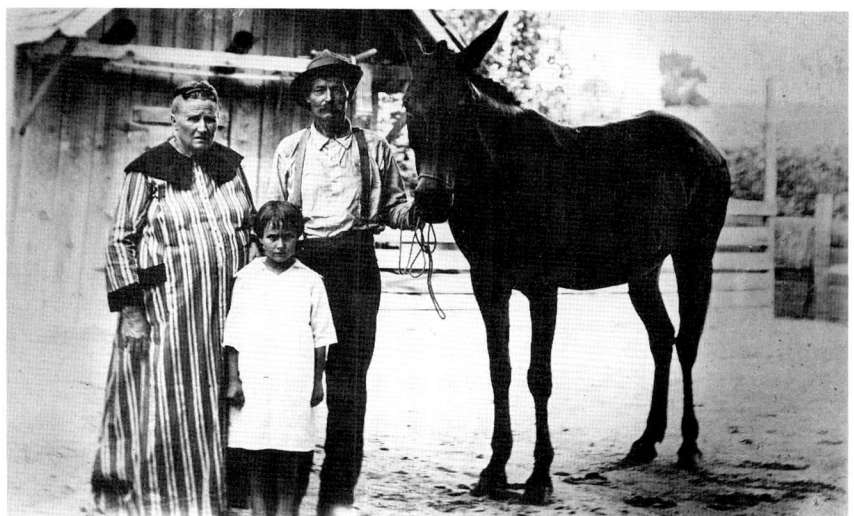

Family with its mule in the barnyard. *Henry York* (1890–1947). Gelatin silver postcard print. Smith County, between 1907 and 1914. Smith County Historical Society Archives.

Young boy feeding chickens from a pail. Henry York (1890–1947). Gelatin silver postcard print. Smith County, between 1907 and 1914. Smith County Historical Society Archives.
York sold postcard photographs for seventy-five cents per dozen.

1900's

1900's

Christmas play at the First Presbyterian Church. *Paul H. Naschke* (1872–1932).
Gelatin silver print. Galveston, Galveston County, 1902 or 1903. Rosenberg Library.

"Texas Brag." *Martin Postcard Company* (firm active ca. 1910).
From a copy negative. Unidentified location, 1909.
Institute of Texan Cultures.

This photograph is an early example of Texas braggadocio. It is the forerunner of the popular "Jackelope" and other postcards that make light of the Texas myth.

Still life of Midland County fruit. *Miller* (active early 1900s).
Gelatin silver print. Midland, Midland County, 1908.
Midland County Museum.

1900's

A meeting of early Texas ranchmen of Tom Green County. *Unidentified photographer.* Gelatin silver print. San Angelo vicinity, Tom Green County, about 1900. Fort Concho Museum.

"Matador Range," Texas. *Erwin Evans Smith* (1886–1947).
Gelatin silver print. Panhandle area, 1909–1910. Erwin E. Smith Collection, Library of Congress.
A trail herd headed for shipment from Lubbock, Texas. The cattle were allowed to drift along fairly slowly as they traveled several days to reach the railroad.

1900's

Daddy, Henry, and Old Boy. *Unidentified photographer.*
Gelatin silver print. San Angelo, Tom Green County, about
1900. Fort Concho Museum.

Photographer with a burro. *J. C. McClure* (active early 1900s).

Gelatin silver print. Possibly Mineral Wells vicinity, Parker County, about 1905. Texas/Dallas History and Archives Division, Dallas Public Library.

1910's

1910's

"Pony stalls at Turkey Tracks Ranch." *Erwin Evans Smith* (1886–1947). Gelatin silver print. Panhandle, 1910. Erwin E. Smith Collection, Library of Congress.

John Morgan Waller. *Unidentified photographer.*
Gelatin silver print. San Angelo, Tom Green County, about 1910. Fort Concho Museum.
Waller (1838–1915) was a veteran of the Civil War.

Studio portrait of a man. *Julius C. Born* (1879–1962).
Modern gelatin silver print from a glass negative. Canadian, Hemphill County, about 1910. Panhandle Plains Museum.

1910's

Miners. *Unidentified photographer.* Collodio-chloride print. Thurber, Erath County, 1910 or before. University of Texas at Arlington.

Thurber is remembered as the only 100 percent union shop town in Texas. The United Mine Workers organized coal miners there in 1903, and State Federation of Labor Secretary C. W. Woodman subsequently set up unions for every other profession, including a union for unskilled workers.

Granite quarry. *Unidentified photographer.* From a copy print. Llano, Llano County, about 1910. Texas State Library.

1910's

The Lone Star Grocery. *Unidentified photographer.*
Gelatin silver print. San Antonio, Bexar County, early 1910s. San Antonio Museum Association.

"Telegraph Poles, Texas, 1915."
Paul Strand (1890–1976).
Gelatin silver print from an enlarged lantern slide.
Unidentified location, 1915. Paul Strand Archive and
Library, Silver Mountain Foundation.

1910's

Halley's Comet as seen in El Paso.
W. F. Stuart (active 1906–1923).

Gelatin silver print. El Paso, El Paso County, May 16, 1910. Museum of New Mexico.

The comet was not bright enough to be clearly photographed. The photographer retouched the negative to make the print look more like the comet appeared to the eye.

153

1910's

Woman and child in a field of bluebonnets. *Unidentified photographer.*
Gelatin silver print. Possibly Austin vicinity, Travis County, about 1910. Texas State Library.
Lupinus texensis, the bluebonnet, was adopted as the state flower on March 7, 1901.

1910's

"Enjoying the oysters right from the shell."
Frank J. Schlueter (1874?-1972).
Gelatin silver print. Near Morgan's Point, Harris County, about 1915. Collection of Colleen Talmadge Claybourn.

1910's

Tight-rope performer and spectators at Mollie Bailey's Circus.
Cecil Bouldin James (1882–1971).
Modern gelatin silver print from the original nitrate negative. Hamilton, Hamilton County, about 1913. Collection of Maxine Havens.

"Resting Meadow, South Texas." *Frank J. Schlueter* (1874?-1972).
Gelatin silver postcard print. Richmond vicinity, Fort Bend County, about 1910.
Fort Bend County Museum.

The University of Texas Medical Department Bacteriological Lab. *Joseph M. Maurer* (1876–1953).

Gelatin silver print. Galveston, Galveston County, about 1910. Moody Medical Library, University of Texas Medical Branch.

The University of Texas Medical Branch was opened in 1891 after a statewide referendum was held to determine the location of the Medical Department.

Boomtown, Goose Creek field. *F. C. Allen* (active 1910s).

Gelatin silver print. Baytown, Harris County, February 1917. Collection of Dorothy Louise Burns.

Oil had been extracted since 1908 in Goose Creek, but the town boomed in 1916 when drillers struck an 8,000-barrel gusher. In 1917, the Simmes-Sinclair Number 11 Sweet produced 35,000 barrels each day. Emmett Albert Sweeney, team pusher for Al Arnell, is on the left.

1910's

Robert Leroy Parker, alias Butch Cassidy, and the Wild Bunch. *Bryant Studio* (firm active ca. 1910).

Gelatin silver print. Fort Worth, Tarrant County, about 1910. Collection of Jimmy Adair.

Cassidy sent a copy of this photograph to the famous detective, Allan Pinkerton, with a note, "Come and get us."

Studio portrait of B. de la Vega.
Unidentified photographer.
Gelatin silver postcard print. Possibly San Antonio, Bexar County, July 1918. Institute of Texan Cultures.

Construction of the Amicable Building. *Fred A. Gildersleeve* (1881?-1958).
Gelatin silver print. Waco, McLennan County, 1910. Texas Collection, Baylor University.

The Amicable Building was the tallest structure west of the Mississippi for many years after it was built. Its 22 stories rise 303 feet from the sidewalk to the top of the flagpole. The building was designed by Sanguinet and Staadts of Fort Worth and was built as the home office of the Amicable Life Insurance Company. In 1965, after Amicable Life merged with the American Life Insurance Company, the building was renamed the ALICO Building.

The Amicable Building. *Fred A. Gildersleeve* (1881?–1958).
Gelatin silver print. Waco, McLennan County, 1911. Texas Collection, Baylor University.

This view showing the newly completed Amicable Building, which remains the central landmark of Waco, is taken looking east from Sixth Street toward City Hall Square.

1910's

Real estate offices of Theodore Koch and Company at Riviera and Riviera Beach. *C. L. Sult and Sons of Corpus Christi* (firm active 1910s).

Hand-tinted gelatin silver print. Riviera, Kleberg County, about 1913. John E. Conner Museum, Texas A&I University.

Koch was the Dutch Consul in Minneapolis, and it was part of his job to keep his eyes open for land in America suitable for settlement by the Dutch. Koch came to Texas to evaluate prospects in the Valley and persuaded the King Ranch to sell him land for Dutch communities. Koch ultimately owned more than 50,000 acres. This photograph is from an album used to promote the community, showing off the landscape and the beachfront.

Return of the 90th Division. *Hugo L. Summerville Studios* (firm active 1910s–1920s).

Gelatin silver print. San Antonio, Bexar County, 1918. Library of the Daughters of the Republic of Texas.

Panorama of Polk Street. *McCormick* (active 1910s).
Gelatin silver print. Amarillo, Potter County and Randall County, 1910. Panhandle Plains Museum.

Using a special "Cirkut" camera that panned across the scene, McCormick was able to look both ways down the center of both these roads.

1910's

Japanese rice farmers.
Unidentified photographer.
Gelatin silver print. Orange, Orange County, 1912. Collection of H. C. Williams.

All along the coast, Japanese immigrants found employment in rice farming.

1910's

18th Division, 19th Infantry, Camp Travis. *Unidentified photographer.* Gelatin silver print. San Antonio, Bexar County, about 1918. Colorado Historical Society.

1910's

1910's

Threshing wheat.
Unidentified photographer
Gelatin silver snapshot print. Cloverdale, possibly Midland County, 1916. Midland County Museum.

1910's

San Antonio messenger boys for the red light district. *Louis Wickes Hine* (1874–1940).
Gelatin silver print. San Antonio, Bexar County, October 1913. Museum of Fine Arts, Houston.
Louis Hine was a teacher of sociology at the Ethical Cultural School in New York when he was hired as an investigator and photographer for the National Child Labor Committee. Using his photographs as illustrations of poor working conditions, the NCLC lobbied for better child labor laws.

Gladys Ahlrich with a dog. *Friederike Recknagel* (1860–1956).
Modern gelatin silver print from the original glass negative. Round Top, Fayette County, about 1911. Collection of E. W. Ahlrich.

Portrait of children with toy piano. *Friederike Recknagel* (1860–1956).
Modern gelatin silver print from the original glass negative. Round Top, Fayette County, about 1916. Collection of E. W. Ahlrich.
Louise Ahlrich, Hedwig Michaelis, Gladys Ahlrich, and Arleen Ahlrich.

Jewish immigrants who just landed at Galveston. *Unidentified photographer.*

Gelatin silver print. Galveston, Galveston County, about 1910. Texas State Library.

Galveston was an important port of entry for immigrants. Between the years 1907 and 1914, the Jewish Immigration Information Bureau, directed by Rabbi Henry Cohen, helped some 10,000 European Jews settle in Texas and the Midwest.

McArthur Cullen Ragsdale reading. *Henry C. Ragsdale* (1883–1963).
Gelatin silver print. San Angelo, Tom Green County, about 1905. Fort Concho Museum.

Photographer and young woman. *Henry York* (1890–1947).
Gelatin silver postcard print. Tyler vicinity, Smith County, about 1910. Smith County Historical Society Archives.

1920's

1920s

Firemen posed with hose and trophy. *Unidentified photographer.*

Gelatin silver print. La Grange, Fayette County, early 1920s. Fayette Heritage Museum/Archives.

Competitions between local fire teams were common in the early part of the twentieth century. This team included George Albrecht, Walter Helmcamp, George Schaefer, and William Johnson.

Gymnastics team at the YMCA. Possibly *Joe D. Litterst* (1896–1949).
Gelatin silver print. Houston, Harris County, early 1920s. Harris County Heritage Society.

172

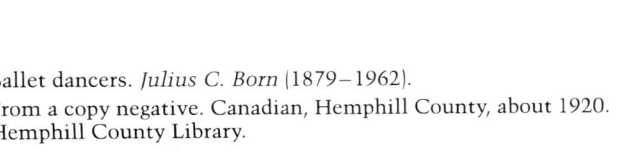

Dance under the canopy of a Magnolia Oil Gasoline Station.
Unidentified photographer.
Gelatin silver print. Fort Worth, Tarrant County, about 1920.
Amon Carter Museum.

This station was part of the Magnolia Building, located on the corner of Third and Commerce.

Ballet dancers. *Julius C. Born (1879–1962).*
From a copy negative. Canadian, Hemphill County, about 1920.
Hemphill County Library.

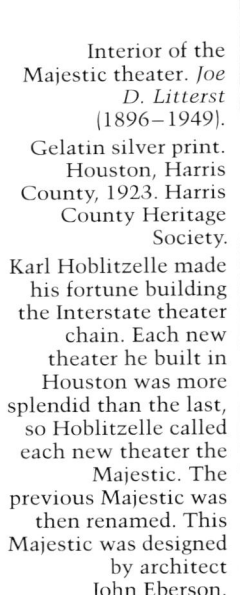

Interior of the Majestic theater. *Joe D. Litterst* (1896–1949). Gelatin silver print. Houston, Harris County, 1923. Harris County Heritage Society.

Karl Hoblitzelle made his fortune building the Interstate theater chain. Each new theater he built in Houston was more splendid than the last, so Hoblitzelle called each new theater the Majestic. The previous Majestic was then renamed. This Majestic was designed by architect John Eberson.

Billboard for the Progress Laundry. *Fred A. Gildersleeve* (1881?–1958).

Modern gelatin silver print from the original glass negative. Waco, McLennan County, about 1920. Texas Collection, Baylor University.

"The Burkburnett oil field." *Underwood and Underwood* (active 1880–1931).

Gelatin silver stereograph. Burkburnett, Wichita County, 1928. Collection of Carol Roark.

1920's

"The biggest airship and the biggest auto in the biggest state."
Unidentified photographer.

Gelatin silver print. Fort Worth, Tarrant County, 1923. Texas Memorial Museum, University of Texas at Austin.

The airship Shenandoah was 700 feet long. It was the first dirigible to cross Texas.

Sheriff Dan Harston and deputies posing with confiscated stills. *Frank Rogers* (active 1910s–1930s).

Modern gelatin silver print made from the original negative. Dallas, Dallas County, mid-1920s. Texas/Dallas History and Archives Division, Dallas Public Library.

Prohibition, the result of the eighteenth amendment to the U.S. constitution, produced a number of bootleggers and speakeasies. Although moonshining is an old Texas tradition, it has always been illegal. During Prohibition, the revenuers stepped up their vigilance.

"Mission Valley school." *Otto Seidel* (1892–1972).
Modern gelatin silver print from the original negative. New Braunfels, Comal County, April 1928. Sophienberg Memorial Association Archives.

Boys scouts holding their scout handbooks. *Unidentified photographer*.
From a copy negative. Greenville, Hunt County, late 1910s or early 1920s. East Texas State University.

1920's

The Desso family in front of its touring car. *Unidentified photographer.*
From a copy print. Beaumont, Jefferson County, about 1920. Tyrrell Historical Library.

"Dallas, Texas from the air."
Keystone View Company
(active 1892–1963).
Gelatin silver stereograph.
Dallas, Dallas County, about 1925. Layland Museum.

Orangefield during the "boom." *Industrial Co.* (firm active 1920s).

Gelatin silver print.
Orangefield, Orange County, 1920. Collection of H. C. Williams.

Orangefield was founded when oil was discovered there in 1913.

1920's

Lone Star Cotton Mills, second floor, east tower. *Harvey Patteson* (active 1920s). Gelatin silver print. San Antonio, Bexar County, July 1921. San Antonio Museum Association.

Baptizing in San Pedro — May 25 1925

1920's

Baptizing in San Pedro Park.
Eugene Omar Goldbeck (b. 1892).
Modern gelatin silver print from the original nitrate Cirkut panorama negative. San Antonio, Bexar County, May 1925. Harry Ransom Humanities Research Center, University of Texas at Austin.

This baptism was a part of a Baptist revival led by John Franklyn Norris (center left). Norris left the General Baptist Convention of Texas to become a leader of the rival Fundamental Baptist churches. He was noted for waging popular campaigns against drinking, horse racing, and the teaching of evolution. His Fort Worth Baptist church was the largest in the world, with a congregation of 8,000.

1920's

Immigration border patrol. *Eugene Omar Goldbeck* (b. 1892).
Modern gelatin silver print made from the original nitrate Cirkut panoramic negative. Laredo, Webb County, 1926. Harry Ransom Humanities Research Center, University of Texas at Austin.

1920's

Third Annual Bathing Girl Revue. *Eugene Omar Goldbeck* (b. 1892).

Modern gelatin silver print made from the original nitrate Cirkut panorama negative. Galveston, Galveston County, May 14, 1922. Harry Ransom Humanities Research Center, University of Texas at Austin.

This annual event drew thousands of Texans to view the contestants in costumes ornately decorated with sea motifs.

1920's

Guards on duty. *A. Klucker.*
Gelatin silver print. Richmond, Fort Bend County, September 1922. Fort Bend County Museum.
The photographer's name is probably a pseudonym to protect his identity.

1920's

"Ned with pig." *Grace Whitt* (1885–1958).
Gelatin silver print. Coke County, about 1920. Collection of Skeet McAuley.

Tassie Harden. *Francis (Frank) King Duncan* (1878–1970). Modern gelatin silver print from the original negative. Marfa, Presidio County, about 1923. Marfa–Presidio County Museum.

Public health clinic. *Francis (Frank) King Duncan (1878–1970).*
Modern gelatin silver print from the original negative. Marfa, Presidio County, about 1925. Marfa-Presidio County Museum.

First Prize, Hemphill County Exhibit, Texas State Fair. *Unidentified photographer.*
Gelatin silver print. Dallas, Dallas County, 1929. Hemphill County Library.

1920s

"Here is Scout Sidney Zinberg, 312 Peach Street, doing his good turn by escorting little Margaret Adams through traffic."
Jack Specht (b. 1896), for the *San Antonio Light*.

Modern gelatin silver print from the original glass negative. San Antonio, Bexar County, February 1925. Institute of Texan Cultures.

"While waiting for The *Light* baseball extra Frank Allison, newsie, hooked his $2 Howe set to the grill [on the *Light* building] in the alley and picked up WCAR, repeating the plays to his friend, Joe Fisher, Alamo Plaza newsie." *Jack Specht* (b. 1896), for the *San Antonio Light*.

Modern gelatin silver print from the original glass negative. San Antonio, Bexar County, October 1925. Institute of Texan Cultures.

"Maybe 'there ain't no flies' on the courthouse, but there will be Saturday when Babe White, human fly, climbs the sides with his bare hands." *Jack Specht* (b. 1896), for the *San Antonio Light*.

Modern gelatin silver print from the original glass negative, San Antonio, Bexar County, April 1925. Institute of Texan Cultures.

"Hayward Thompson, 'blindfold wizard,' who sees with his skin, is telling Mayor John W. Tobin the color and texture of his clothing." *Jack Specht* (b. 1896), for the *San Antonio Light*.

Modern gelatin silver print from the original glass negative. San Antonio, Bexar County, December 1925. Institute of Texan Cultures.

"Thompson, once totally blind, is going to drive an automobile down Houston Street, blindfolded . . . repeating a stunt he has done some 207 times without mishap." The photograph was made on Navarro Street, with Dorothy Morris, Secretary of the San Antonio Heart Association, looking on.

Officers of the Daughters of the Republic of Texas. *Hugo L. Summerville Studios* (firm active 1910s—1920s).

Modern gelatin silver print from the original nitrate negative. San Antonio, Bexar County, 1925. Harry Ransom Humanities Research Center, University of Texas at Austin.

The Alamo, which serves as a backdrop for this picture, was restored through the efforts of the Daughters of the Republic of Texas. They continue to maintain the building and to operate a museum and research library on the Alamo grounds.

Storefront of Seidel's studio. *Otto Seidel* (1892–1972).

Modern gelatin silver print from the original safety negative. New Braunfels, Comal County, November 1929. Sophienberg Memorial Association Archives.

1930's

1930's

Square dancing on a wagon sheet. *Ray Rector* (1884–1933).

Modern gelatin silver print from the original nitrate negative. SMS Flat Top Ranch, Stamford vicinity, Jones County, about 1930. Harry Ransom Humanities Research Center, University of Texas at Austin.

The wagon sheet was used as a makeshift floor to keep the dry dust from raising a cloud. The fiddler is John Selmon; the women are Mrs. Owens, Mrs. Weathers, and Mrs. Rector, the wife of the photographer.

"Soda Jerker flipping ice cream into a malted milk shaker."
Russell Lee (b. 1903).
Modern gelatin silver print from the original safety negative.
Corpus Christi, Nueces County, February 1939.
Farm Security Administration Collection, Library of Congress.

1930's

"Farm Security Administration clients at home." *Russell Lee* (b. 1903).
Modern gelatin silver print from the original safety negative. Hidalgo County, 1939. Farm Security Administration Collection, Library of Congress.

Rex Tugwell, the Assistant Secretary of Agriculture for Franklin Delano Roosevelt and a part of the original "Brain Trust," had difficulty getting Congress to understand the plight of the farmer during the Depression. Tugwell hired Roy Stryker, a professor of economics at Columbia University, to head a project that would "show the city people what it's like to live on a farm." Stryker's team of photographers made more than 170,000 photographs for the Farm Security Administration that document rural American life during the Depression.

Couple in riding outfits. *Gittings Studio, Dallas* (founded 1929).
From a copy of a gelatin silver print. Dallas, Dallas County, about 1932.
David R. Godine, Publishers.

Portrait of two women and a child. *Harry Forrest Annas* (1897–1908).
From a copy of a gelatin silver print. Lockhart, Caldwell County, about 1930. David R. Godine, Publishers.

Home portrait of father and child. *Gittings Studio, Houston* (founded 1929).
From a copy of a gelatin silver print. Houston, Harris County, about 1930. David R. Godine, Publishers.

Mother photographing her children at a motor hotel. *Biggs* (active 1930s). Modern gelatin silver print from the original negative. Possibly Dallas, Dallas County, 1932. Texas/Dallas History and Archives Division, Dallas Public Library.

Fashion photograph made for Neiman-Marcus at Dallas Country Club. *Biggs* (active 1930s).
Gelatin silver print. Dallas, Dallas County, 1934. Texas/Dallas History and Archives Division, the Dallas Public Library

1930's

Emma Tenayuca leading workers during the pecan shellers' strike. *Unidentified photographer.*

Modern print from the original safety negative. San Antonio, Bexar County, 1938. Institute of Texan Cultures.

Pecan shellers, who were predominantly Mexican-Americans, worked a 54-hour week for $3. The workers were concerned about losing their jobs because of the introduction of mechanical shellers.

Crowds of unemployed at the Texas Furniture Company. *Unidentified photographer* for the *San Antonio Light*.

Modern gelatin silver print from the original glass negative. San Antonio, Bexar County, about 1933. Institute of Texan Cultures.

1930's

Orchestra Typica.
Unidentified photographer.
Gelatin silver print.
San Antonio, Bexar County, 1936.
National Archives.

The Works Progress Administration funded many orchestras and bands around the nation to provide both jobs and psychological relief from the Depression.

1930's

Eugene Permanent Wave Shop. *Unidentified photographer.*
Modern gelatin silver print from the original glass negative. Corpus Christi, February 1934. Harry Ransom Humanities Research Center, University of Texas at Austin.

Window display for the Texas Centennial. *Ellison Studios* (founded 1900).
Gelatin silver print. Austin, Travis County, 1936. Austin History Center.

Jane and Ed Alexander with their dog, Hound.
Gladys Dotson Alexander (b. 1900).
Gelatin silver print. Uvalde, Edwards County, 1935.
Collection of Jane Alexander Knapik.

The Alexanders were on their way to school when this photograph was made.

1930's

"A sleeper plane at the Fort Worth Municipal Airport, built by the Public Works Administration." *Unidentified photographer.* Gelatin silver print. Fort Worth, Tarrant County, 1932–1936. National Archives.

Governor James Allred trying on a pair of boots to begin the Texas Centennial. *Ellison Studios* (founded 1900).
Gelatin silver print. Austin, Travis County, 1936. Austin History Center.

Sculpting statuary for the Centennial Exposition.
Unidentified photographer.
Modern gelatin silver print from the original negative. Dallas, Dallas County, 1936. Texas/Dallas History and Archives Division, Dallas Public Library.
The buildings originally erected for the Centennial celebration in 1936 are among the finest examples of Art Deco architecture in the state. They are still standing on the State Fair grounds.

1930's

"Farm abandoned in 1937 in the cold water district." *Dorothea Lange* (1895–1965).
Modern gelatin silver print from the original safety negative. Dalhart vicinity, Dallam County, June 1938. Farm Security Administration Collection, Library of Congress.

"Wife of a migratory worker with three children." *Dorothea Lange* (1895–1965).

Modern gelatin silver print from the original safety negative. Childress vicinity, Childress County, 1938. Farm Security Administration Collection, Library of Congress.

Nettie Featherston, the woman in this picture, told the photographer, "You can't get no relief here until you've lived here a year. This country's a hard country. They won't help bury you here. If you die, you're dead—that's all."

"Dust Storm." *Arthur Rothstein* (b. 1915).
Modern gelatin silver print from the original safety negative. Amarillo, Potter County, April 1936. Farm Security Administration Collection, Library of Congress.

"Dust storm approaching." *Unidentified photographer.*
Modern gelatin silver print from the original safety negative. Spearman, Hansford County, April 1935. Texas Collection, Baylor University.

1930's

"Migrant mother with children." *Russell Lee* (b. 1903).
Modern gelatin silver print from the original safety negative. Weslaco, Hidalgo County, February 1939. Farm Security Administration Collection, Library of Congress.

"Migrant cotton pickers at lunch time." *Dorothea Lange* (1895–1965).
Modern gelatin silver print from the safety negative. Robstown, Nueces County, August 1936. Farm Security Administration Collection, Library of Congress.

Black delegates to the American Legion National Convention. *Crown Art Photo* (firm active 1930s).

Gelatin silver print. San Antonio, Bexar County, about 1938. Barker Texas History Center, University of Texas at Austin.

Betty Simmons. *Unidentified photographer.*

Gelatin silver print. San Antonio, Bexar County, 1937. Houston Metropolitan Research Center, Houston Public Library.

Simmons was formerly a slave in the Beaumont area. Her photograph is one of a series of portraits of former slaves made for the Texas Works Progress Administration.

1930's

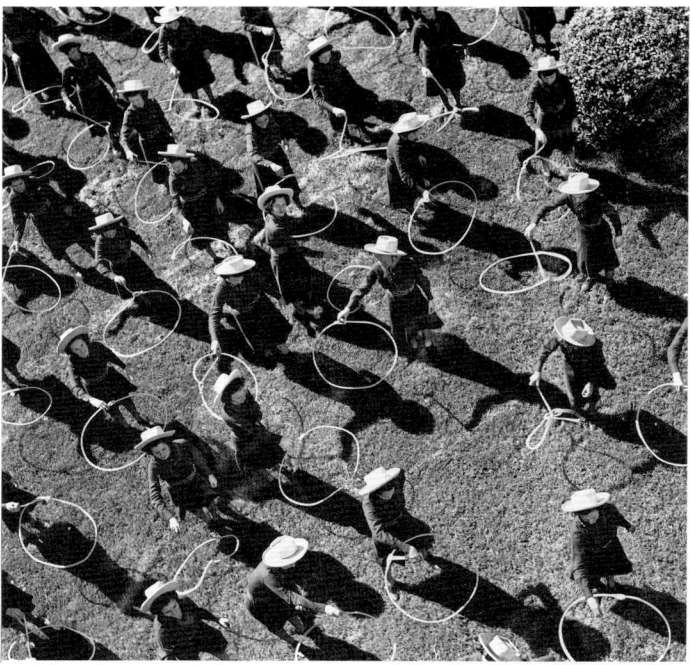
Lasso girls of Thomas Jefferson High School. *Fritz Henle* (b. 1909). Gelatin silver print. Kilgore, Rusk County, 1938. Collection of the photographer.

Studio portrait of two young women. *Jno P. Trlica* (1882–1978). Modern gelatin silver print from the original glass negative. Granger, Williamson County, 1930. Harry Ransom Humanities Research Center, University of Texas at Austin.

"Ladies of pleasure join the boom at Freer, when the money from oil begins to flow."
Carl Mydans (b. 1907), for *LIFE*.
Gelatin silver print. Freer, Duval County, March 1937. *LIFE* Magazine.

1930's

"Loading dock of a flour mill." *Russell Lee* (b. 1903).
Modern gelatin silver print from the original safety negative.
Houston, Harris County, October 1939. Farm Security
Administration Collection, Library of Congress.

"The Mexican section. Front entrance to Mexican home. This is
homemade hand work." *Russell Lee* (b. 1903).
Modern gelatin silver print from the original safety negative. San Antonio,
Bexar County, March 1939. Farm Security Administration Collection,
Library of Congress.

Street scene and storefronts. *Russell Lee* (b. 1903).
Modern gelatin silver print from the nitrate negative. Waco, McLennan County, 1939. Farm Security Administration Collection, Library of Congress.

"Streetscene." *Russell Lee* (b. 1903).
Modern gelatin silver print from the original safety negative. San Augustine, San Augustine County, April 1939. Farm Security Administration Collection, Library of Congress.

1930's

"Mexican Grave."
Russell Lee (b. 1903).
Modern gelatin silver print from the original safety negative. Raymondville, Willacy County, February 1939. Farm Security Administration Collection, Library of Congress.

"Mexican cattle entering Eagle Pass, Texas." *Carl Mydans* (b. 1907), for *LIFE*. Gelatin silver print. Eagle Pass, Maverick County, 1937. *LIFE* Magazine.

1930's

"Derricks in the residential section."
Russell Lee (b. 1903).

Modern gelatin silver print from the original safety negative. Kilgore, Rusk County, 1939. Farm Security Administration Collection, Library of Congress.

 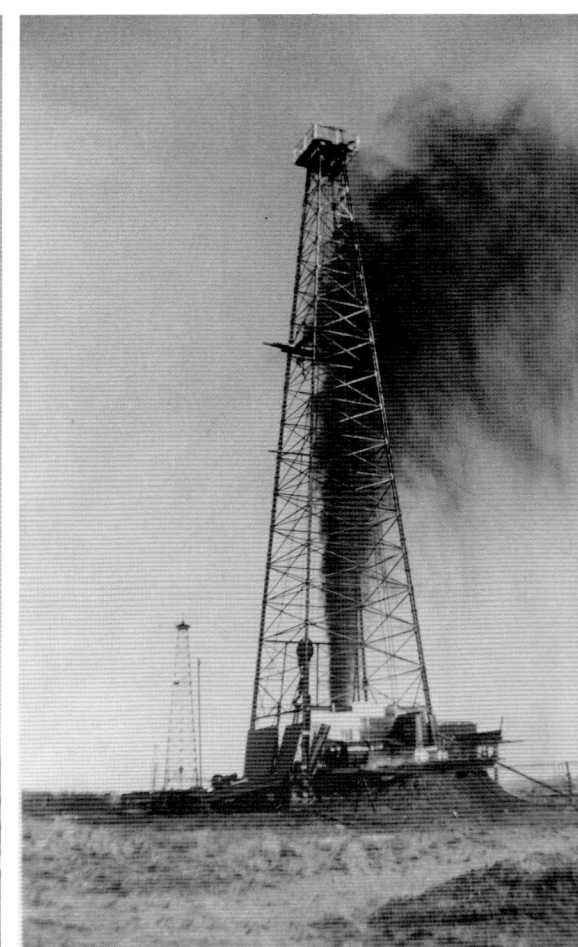

"This well paid off the bank debt." *Vincent C. Perini, Jr.* (1895–1965).

Gelatin silver prints. Ward County, 1936. Collection of Charles W. Perini.

The Hathaway well blowing. The pool on this well helped make Sid Richardson wealthy, according to the caption on the envelope in which these photographs were stored.

1930's

1930's

"Roustabouts: Freer Texas." *Carl Mydans* (b. 1907), for *LIFE*.
Gelatin silver print. Freer, Duval County, March 1937. *LIFE* Magazine.

"A day in the life of Vice-President Garner at his home in Uvalde, Texas."
James F. Laughead (1916–1979).
Modern gelatin silver print from the original safety negative. Uvalde, Uvalde County, mid-1930s. Bradley Photographers.

1930's

Men's clothier fashion window. *Otto Seidel* (1892–1972). Modern gelatin silver print from the original negative. New Braunfels, Comal County, 1934. Sophienberg Memorial Association Archives.

Weighing cotton picked in a day. *James F. Laughead* (1916–1979).

Modern gelatin silver print from the original safety negative. The Valley, possibly Uvalde vicinity, Uvalde County, September or October 1939. Bradley Photographers.

1930's

"A Mexican family, having tried Texas, returns to Mexico." *Wilfred Dudley Smithers* (1895–1981).

Modern gelatin silver print from the original negative. Rio Grande Valley, 1930. Harry Ransom Humanities Research Center, University of Texas at Austin.

Pablo Baiza said he returned to Mexico with his wife, Nona, and his family after being harassed by Texas officers.

Joe Litterst and his camera reflected in a mirrored ball. *Joe D. Litterst* (1896–1949).

Gelatin silver print. Houston, Harris County, about 1930. Harris County Heritage Society.

1940's

1940's

Vaquero child learning to throw a loop. *Toni Frissell* (b.1907).
Gelatin silver print. King Ranch, Kleberg County, early 1940s. Toni Frissell Collection, Library of Congress.

"Clarence Hailey Long goes to town." *Leonard McCombe* (b. 1923), for *LIFE*.
Modern gelatin silver print from the original negative. Possibly Amarillo, Potter County, May 1949. *LIFE* Magazine.

"Cattlemen at an auction of prize beef steers and breeding stock at the San Angelo Fat Stock show." *Russell Lee* (b. 1903).

Modern gelatin silver print from the original safety negative. San Angelo, Tom Green County, March 1940. Farm Security Administration Collection, Library of Congress.

1940's

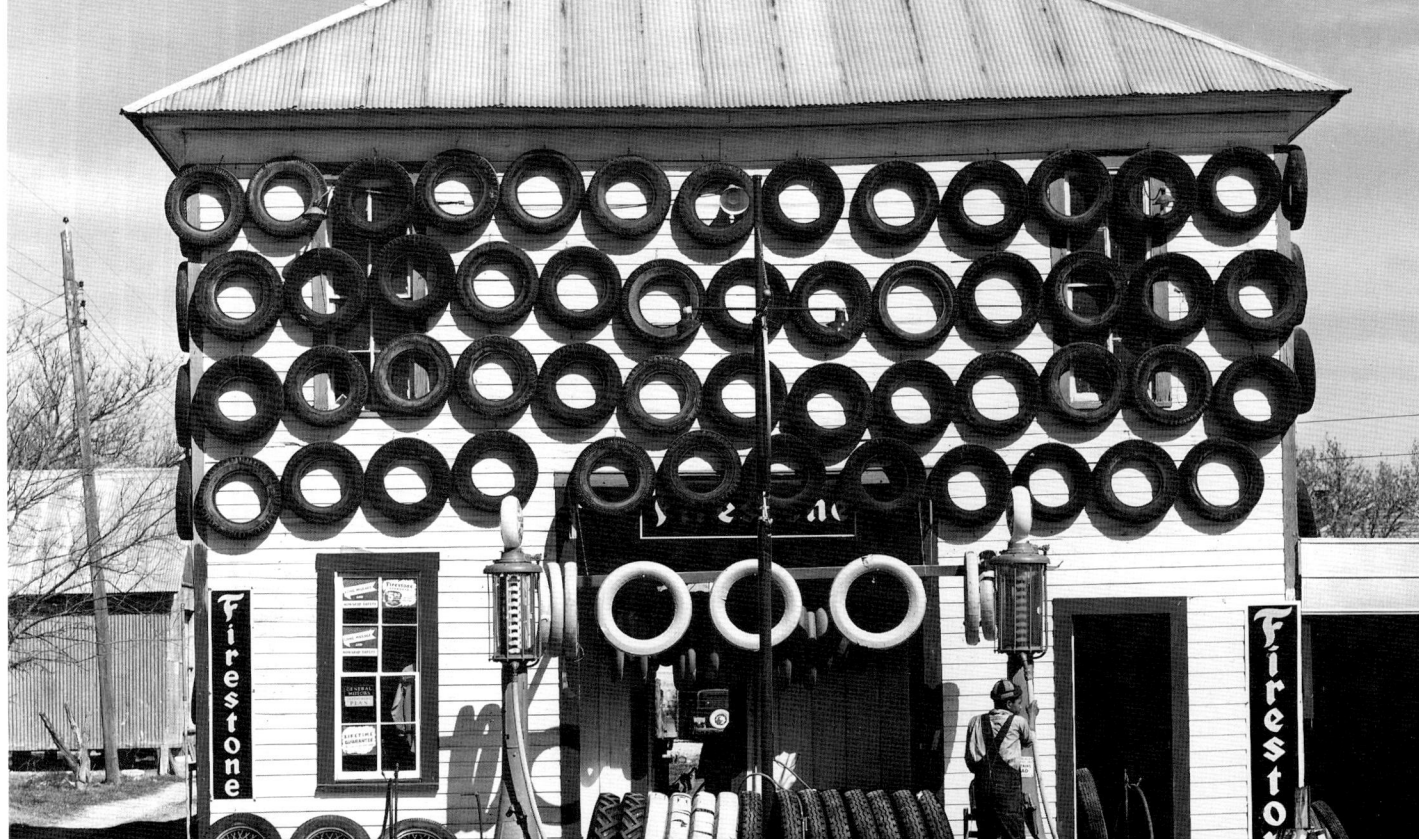

"Second hand tires displayed for sale." *Russell Lee* (b. 1903). Modern gelatin silver print from the original safety negative. San Marcos, Hays County, March 1940. Farm Security Administration Collection, Library of Congress.

"Feed Store." *Esther Bubley* (b. 1921). Modern gelatin silver print from the original safety negative. Tomball, Harris County, May 1945. Standard Oil (New Jersey) Collection, University of Louisville Photographic Archives.

After his work with the Farm Security Administration, Roy Stryker was hired by the Standard Oil Company to promote an image of the oil industry's positive effects on American society. Stryker assembled a team of photographers, many of whom had also worked on the FSA project. These photographs form a document that stresses the same human theme of the FSA pictures, but in contrast shows a prospering America.

229

1940's

"The courthouse square on Saturday afternoon." *John Vachon* (1914–1975). Modern gelatin silver print from the original safety negative. San Augustine, San Augustine County, April 1943. Office of War Information Collection, Library of Congress.

"Financial Center of Midland." *Cornell Capa* (b. 1918), for *LIFE*.
Gelatin silver print. Midland, Midland County, 1940s. *LIFE* Magazine.
The lobby of the Scharbauer Hotel served as an informal "stock exchange" where $50 million worth of business was done each year. Millionaires included in the scene are Jack Wilkinson and Tom Nance (couch, foreground), Joe Crump (background), and Hal Peck (right background).

"Noble Holt Ranch. The line camp at the ranch has no electricity. Gene and Willie Bishop eat their evening meal by kerosene lamp light." *Esther Bubley* (b. 1921).

Modern gelatin silver print from the original safety negative. Near Dryden, Terrell County, September 1945. Standard Oil (New Jersey) Collection, University of Louisville Photographic Archives.

According to the photographer, the couple planned to make a living by writing and selling their autobiography. They were divorced several years after this photograph was made.

1940's

"Bring your pots and pan Hitler." *C. W. Ratliff* (active 1940s).

Modern gelatin silver print from the original negative. Lubbock, Lubbock County, about 1942. Southwest Collection, Texas Tech University.

This was one of many scrap metal drives carried on during World War II.

Martin Dies speaking. *Unidentified photographer.* Gelatin silver print. Possibly San Antonio, Bexar County, about 1940. Sam Houston Regional Library and Research Center.

Dies (1901–1972) represented the Second District in the United States House of Representatives from 1931 to 1945. He established the House Un-American Activities Committee in 1938, which he chaired until 1945.

1940's

Mrs. Yard with her dog. *Howard's Studio* (founded ca. 1930s).
Modern gelatin silver print from the original negative. Pecos, Reeves County, about 1940. Howard's Studio.

Mr. and Mrs. Fry. *Edward Weston* (1886–1958).
Gelatin silver print. Austin, Travis County, 1941. Center for Creative Photography, University of Arizona.

Carpenter's pickets. *C. W. Ratliff* (active 1940s).
Modern gelatin silver print from the original negative. Lubbock, Lubbock County, about 1940. Southwest Collection, Texas Tech University.

Construction of the Driscoll Hotel. *Unidentified photographer.*
Gelatin silver print. Corpus Christi, Nueces County, early 1940s.
Corpus Christi Caller-Times.

1940's

Otis and Iris Davis, with their sons, William and Paul. *Unidentified photographer.*
Modern gelatin silver print from the original safety negative. Corpus Christi, Nueces County, 1941. Collection of Iris C. Davis.

"Harvey Gunter, a mechanic at the E. I. du Pont Sabine River Works turns to car tinkering when off the Job." *Unidentified photographer*, for *DuPont Better Living*.
Gelatin silver print. Sabine, Jefferson County, 1949. National Archives.
A photograph from the files of the United States Information Agency, this photograph and others like it were used to promote a positive image of America.

Hunters with deer. *C. W. Ratliff* (active 1940s).

Modern gelatin silver print from the original negative. Lubbock, Lubbock County, 1941. Southwest Collection, Texas Tech University.

Lyndon Johnson campaigning in the Texas Hill Country. *Jimmie A. Dodd* (1917–1984).

Modern gelatin silver print from the original negative. Possibly Kerrville, Kerr County, 1948. Barker Texas History Center, University of Texas at Austin.

Johnson (1908–1973) was the first politician to use a helicopter in a political campaign. In five weeks Johnson made 370 stops, including appearances over the rallies of his opponent, Coke Stevenson.

1940's

"Gulf Oil, Port Arthur." *Edward Weston* (1886–1958). Gelatin silver print. Port Arthur, Jefferson County, 1941. Amon Carter Museum.

"Light ends fractionators with Hortonspheres for butadiene in foreground." *Harold Corsini* (b. 1919).

Gelatin silver print. Baytown, Harris County, June 1946. Standard Oil (New Jersey) Collection, University of Louisville Photographic Archives.

1940's

Hispanic wedding party. *Otto Seidel* (1892–1972).
Modern gelatin silver print from the original negative. New Braunfels, Comal County, 1942. Sophienberg Memorial Association Archives.

Family portrait. *Unidentified photographer.*
Gelatin silver print. Austin, Travis County, 1942. Pan American Union Collection, Library of Congress.

The caption on the photograph mount: "This man is an applicant for a home in the American-Mexican US housing project. He supports his widowed sister and her six children on WPA salary of $38 per month. The Austin Housing Authority decided not to let these people live in the 'Jim Crow' housing project because their monthly income was too low to assure their being regular paying tenants."

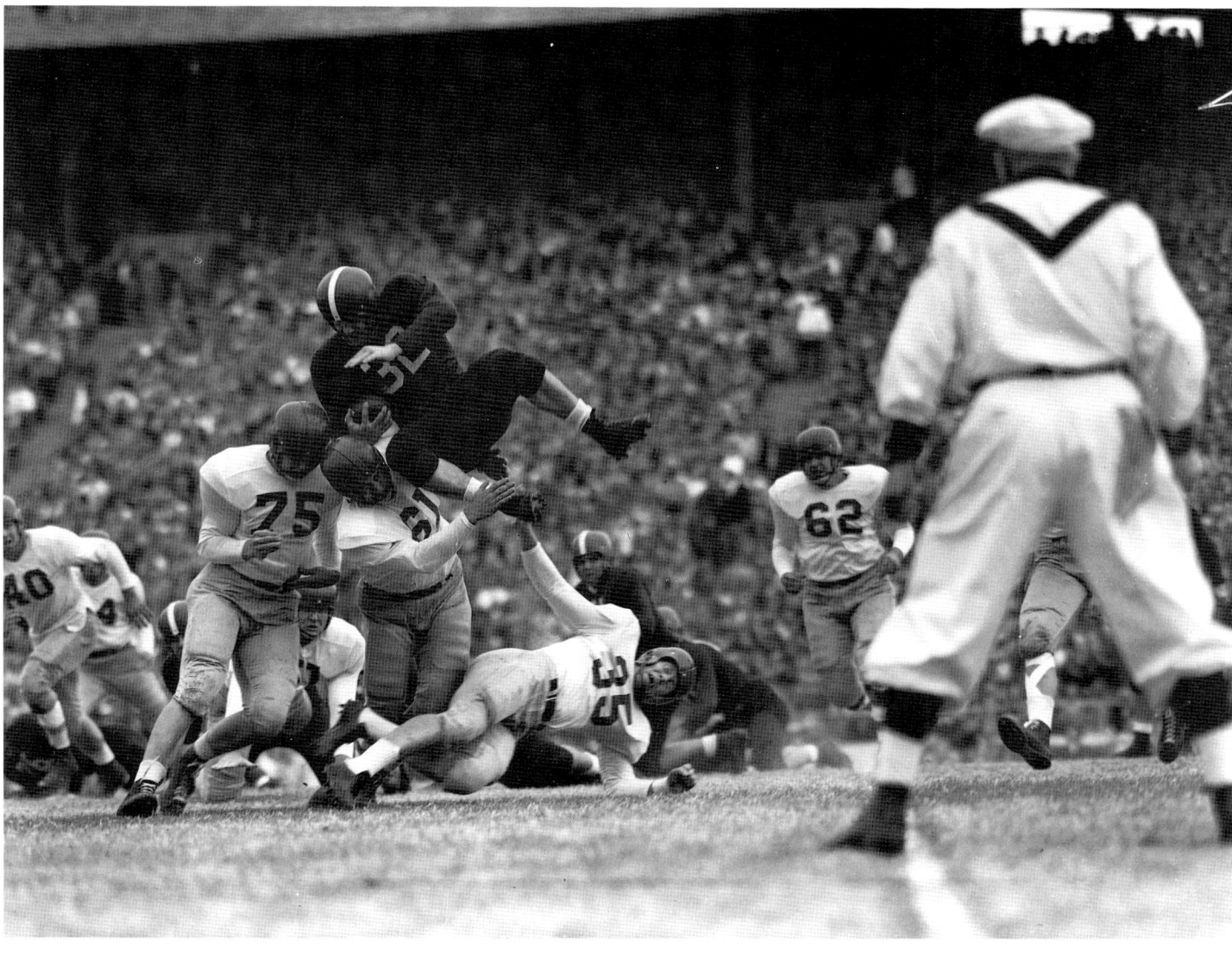

"Southern Methodist University versus Texas Christian University." *Johnny Hayes* (active 1940–1960). Modern gelatin silver print from the original negative. Dallas, Dallas County, 1946. Texas/Dallas History and Archives Division, Dallas Public Library.

SMU won this home game 30–13.

1940's

"No Mexican children allowed." *Unidentified photographer*. Gelatin silver print. Possibly Austin, Travis County, 1942. Pan American Union Collection, Library of Congress.

The caption on the photograph mount: "This typical U.S. Housing Project in Texas is for White Texans only. A strict 'Jim Crow' system governs the selection of sites for U.S. financed housing projects in this state. Each Texas town usually has at least three projects—one for Aryans, one for Negroes, and one for Mexicans."

"A farm."
John Vachon
(1914–1975).
Modern gelatin silver print from the original safety negative. Victoria County, May 1943. Office of War Information Collection, Library of Congress.

1940s

"The Rio Grande yields its surplus to the sea." *Laura Gilpin* (1891–1979).
Gelatin silver print. Texas/Mexico border, Cameron County, February 1947. Amon Carter Museum.

"Burro Mesa and the Chisos Mountains, Big Bend National Park, Texas, 1942." *Ansel Adams* (1902–1983). Gelatin silver print. Big Bend National Park, Brewster County, 1942. Ansel Adams Publishing Rights Trust.

1940's

1940's

"Bubble-Gum King." *Cornell Capa* (b. 1918), for *LIFE*.
Gelatin silver print. McAllen, Hidalgo County, January 1947.
LIFE Magazine.
The original caption reads: "In his office . . . Andrew J. Paris pensively snaps his gum into a perfect bubble almost big enough to hide his moustache. . . . This year Mr. Paris plans to dump some 5,000 tons of bubble gum on the market and thereby win himself a temporary corner on a business that will make money as long as kids from 6 to 16 are able to chew."

"Defending her title as the nation's top 'Glamburger Girl.'"
Unidentified photographer.
Gelatin silver print. Galveston, Galveston County, 1943.
Rosenberg Library.
The "Glamburger Girl" is Jeanette Deal of Houston.

"Children watching electric trains in a downtown store window."
Russell Lee (b. 1903).

Gelatin silver print. Harlingen, Cameron County, 1947. Standard Oil (New Jersey) Collection, University of Louisville Photographic Archives.

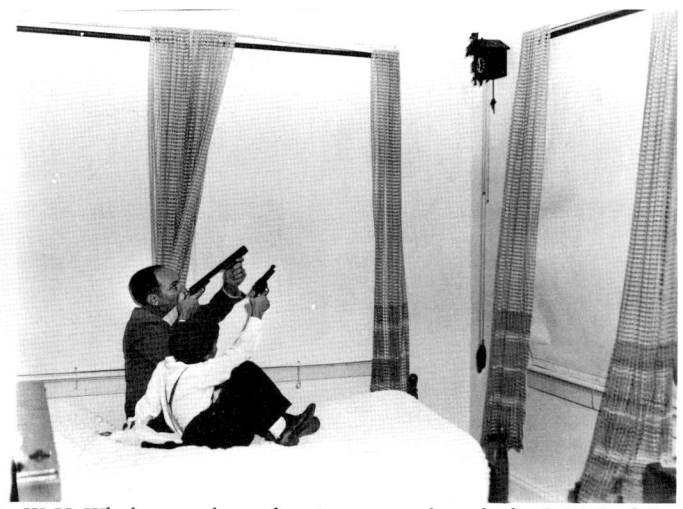

Dr. W. H. Whyburn and son shooting at a cuckoo clock. *C. W. Ratliff* (active 1940s).

Modern gelatin silver print from the original negative. Lubbock, Lubbock County, September 1944. Southwest Collection, Texas Tech University.

Dr. Whyburn was the new president of Texas Tech University.

1940's

"V-E Day. Mayor Cecil Faris proclaims V-E Day to be an official holiday." *Esther Bubley* (b. 1921). Gelatin silver print. Tomball, Harris County, 1945. Standard Oil (New Jersey) Collection, University of Louisville Photographic Archives.

"V-J Day." *The Hayes* (firm active 1930s–1960s), for the *Dallas Times-Herald*. Gelatin silver print. Dallas, August 1945. Texas/Dallas History and Archives Division, Dallas Public Library

1940s

"Baptist church. Some members of the choir." *Esther Bubley* (b. 1921).

Gelatin silver print. Tomball, Harris County, May 1945. Standard Oil (New Jersey) Collection, University of Louisville Photographic Archives.

Mildred McGowan, Noreen Cannon, F. K. Rose, and C. H. Shaw.

"Math exhibition given by M. M. Ferguson before faculty [of] Pecos High School." *Howard's Studio* (founded ca. 1930s).

Modern gelatin silver print from the original negative. Pecos, Reeves County, April 24, 1946. Howard's Studio.

Demonstration of math wizardry by Manton M. Ferguson, author of *Business Mathematics Modernized*. Ferguson's letterhead carries the legend, "Forty years' research on business arithmetic: results, simple understandable sciences heretofore totally unknown."

"Shirley Rylander curling her hair in front of mirror."
Morris Engel (b. 1918).
Gelatin silver print. Buda, Hays County, October 1949.
Amon Carter Museum.

"Top of Stuart Haby Jr.'s dresser."
Esther Bubley (b. 1921).
Modern gelatin silver print from the original safety negative Bandera County, 1945. Standard Oil (New Jersey) Collection, University of Louisville Photographic Archives.

1940's

Living insignia made in honor of the Air Force's 40th anniversary. *Eugene Omar Goldbeck* (b. 1892).

Modern contact print from the original glass negative. Lackland Air Force Base, San Antonio, Bexar County, July 1947. Harry Ransom Humanities Research Center, University of Texas at Austin.

There are 21,765 men in this photograph. Most men wore their uniforms, but others wore only T-shirts to make the pattern of the insignia. Goldbeck wanted every face to be equally spaced in the photograph, so he increased the distance between ranks from only sixteen inches in front to twenty-six feet in the rear. Only ten percent of the men in the photograph are in the bottom half of the insignia.

"Estate surrounded by citrus trees. Young trees surround the landscaped grounds— two miles north of Weslaco." *Russell Lee* (b. 1903).
Gelatin silver print. North of Weslaco, Hidalgo County, January 1948. Standard Oil (New Jersey) Collection, University of Louisville Photographic Archives.

1940's

Spectators watching firemen extinguish a fire at the Turf Building. *Witwer Studios* (firm active 1940s).
Gelatin silver print. Galveston, Galveston County, 1948. Rosenberg Library.

"Oil Tanks with Bridge." *Carlotta Corpron* (b. 1901).
Gelatin silver print. Jefferson vicinity, Marion County, about 1942. Amon Carter Museum.

Wedding portrait. *Gittings Studios* (founded 1929).
From a copy print. Unidentified location, 1949.
Texas Monthly.

1940's

"Little Left." Aftermath of the Texas City Explosion. *Ed Miley* (active 1940s). Gelatin silver print. Texas City, Galveston County, April 16, 1947. Rosenberg Library.

On April 16, 1947, the French liner *Grandcamp* was berthed opposite the Monsanto refinery's docks when fire broke out on board the ship. As the ship was being towed out to sea, its cargo of ammonium nitrate exploded. The blast ignited the benzol storage tanks at the Monsanto plant and leveled warehouses, laboratories, and offices. More than 200 people lost their lives as a result of the explosion. The explosion caused power failures in Houston, and Monsanto pilots reported that the smoke cloud from the fires extended to the southern border of Missouri.

"Searching in the Ruins." Aftermath of the Texas City Explosion. *Unidentified photographer.*
Gelatin silver postcard print. Texas City, Galveston County, April 16, 1948. Rosenberg Library.

1940s

"Truck driver asleep in cab of his truck." *Russell Lee* (b. 1903). Gelatin silver print. Vernon, Wilbarger County, June 1949. Standard Oil (New Jersey) Collection, University of Louisville Photographic Archives.

"Beside chuckwagon, in fading light, Clarence Hailey Long reads a western magazine."
Leonard McCombe (b. 1923), for *LIFE*.
Gelatin silver print. Panhandle, Armstrong, Donley, or Briscoe County, 1949. *LIFE* Magazine.
Long was the foreman of the JA Ranch, which covered 320,000 acres.

1950's

1950's

"Ripper Van Winkle II's 3rd birthday party." *James T. Bradley* (b. 1922).
Modern gelatin silver print from the original safety negative. Dallas, Dallas County, 1950. Bradley Photography.

"I was a Communist for the F.B.I." *The Hayes* (firm active 1930s–1960s), for the *Dallas Times-Herald*.
Gelatin silver print. Dallas, Dallas County, May 1951. Texas/Dallas History and Archives Division, Dallas Public Library.

This Warner Brothers film was based on the memoirs of Matt Cvetic, who did undercover work for the F.B.I. as a plant in a Communist group. Bosley Crowther, reviewing the film for the *New York Times*, commented, ". . . in glibly detailing how the Communists foment radical hate and labor unrest in this country, it colors its scenes so luridly that the susceptible in the audience might catch a hint that most Negroes and most laborers are 'pinks.'"

Ghetto homes with Dallas skyline in background. *Unidentified photographer.*
Gelatin silver print. Dallas, Dallas County, early 1950s. Texas/Dallas History and Archives Division, Dallas Public Library.

Prudential Building. *Robert Frank* (b. 1924).
Gelatin silver print. Houston, Harris County, 1955–1956. Collection of the photographer.

1950's

Segregated clinic.
Watkins
(active 1950s).
Gelatin silver print.
Palestine, Anderson
County, early 1950s.
Houston Metropolitan
Research Center,
Houston Public
Library.

Big Bend. *Eliot Porter* (b. 1901).

Gelatin silver print. Big Bend, Brewster County, 1950. Collection of the photographer.

1950's

"Panelled Luminosity— Number 1."
Clarence John Laughlin (1905–1985), for *LIFE*. Gelatin silver print. Galveston, Galveston County, September 1959. Historic New Orleans Collection.

The B'nai Israel Synagogue, on 22nd Street between Avenue H and Avenue I (Sealy Street). The architect was Fred Stewart, and changes were made in 1890 under the direction of Nicholas Clayton. The synagogue was converted to a Masonic temple in 1953.

Lakewood Theater.
George McAfee
(active 1950s).
Gelatin silver print.
Dallas, Dallas County,
about 1950. Texas/
Dallas History and
Archives Division,
Dallas Public Library.

1950's

Hats on chest top. *Robert Frank* (b. 1924).
Gelatin silver print. Houston, Harris County, 1955–1956. Collection of the photographer.

"Hats in chair—Brazos River Valley 1956." *Russell Lee* (b. 1903).
Gelatin silver print. Brazos River Valley, 1956. Collection of the photographer.

Howard Behrent family portrait, Christmas.
Carol Dryden (1918–1972).
Gelatin silver print. Falfurrias, Brooks County, December 1951. Heritage Museum of Falfurrias.
This photograph was used as the Behrent family Christmas card.

1950's

Dale Evans and Roy Rogers. *Unidentified photographer.* Gelatin silver print. Commerce, Hunt County, 1956. Commerce Local History Collection, Commerce Public Library.

Roy Rogers and Dale Evans, the "King and Queen of cowboys," were in Commerce visiting with some of the children of the W. J. Wheeler Elementary School, winner of the Roy Rogers National Safety Contest Award for 1955.

The Cotton Bowl. *The Hayes* (firm active 1930s–1960s), for the *Dallas Times-Herald*.
Gelatin silver print. Dallas, Dallas County, 1950s. Texas/Dallas History and Archives Division, Dallas Public Library.

Evangelist. *Harry Forrest Annas* (1897–1980).
From a copy of a gelatin silver print. Lockhart, Caldwell County, 1950s. David R. Godine, Publishers.

1950's

"New Rich." *Dan Weiner* (1919–1959), for *Fortune*.
Gelatin silver print. Waco, McLennan County, January 1952.
Collection of Sandra Weiner.
Ross Sams made his fortune as a manufacturer of church furnishings.

U.S. 90, en route to Del Rio, Texas. *Robert Frank* (b. 1924).
Gelatin silver print. Del Rio vicinity, Val Verde County, 1955–1956.
Museum of Fine Arts, Houston.

Robert Dixon and his car. *Unidentified photographer.*
Gelatin silver print. Houston, Harris County, 1952. Harris County Heritage Society.

"Seven thousand engines at Ford assembly plant." *Clint Grant* (active 1950s).
Gelatin silver print. East Dallas, Dallas County, about 1950. Texas/Dallas History and Archives Division, Dallas Public Library.

1950's

Topper hamburgers. *George McAfee* (active 1950s). Gelatin silver print. Dallas, Dallas County, about 1950. Texas/Dallas History and Archives Division, Dallas Public Library.

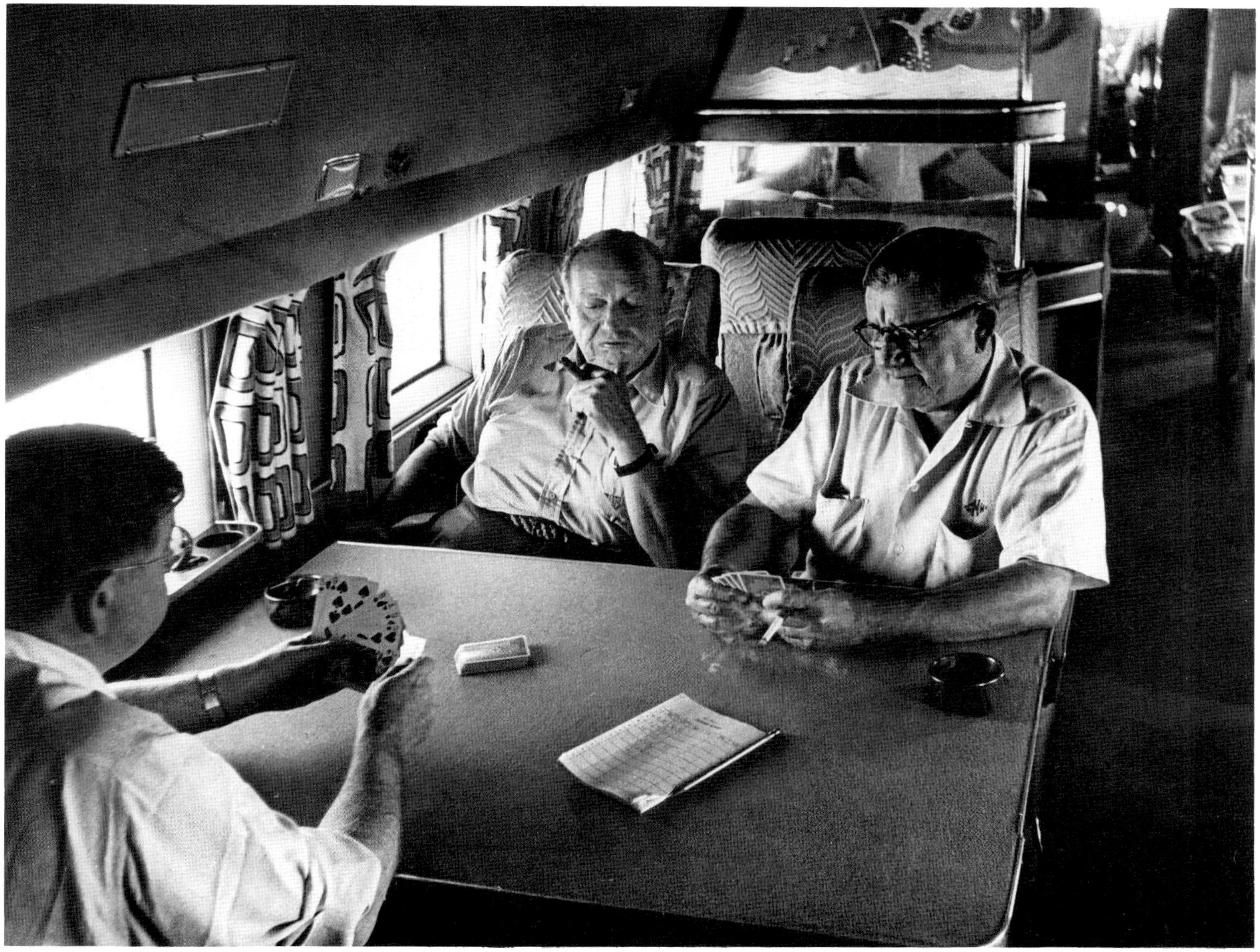

Clint Murchison, Sid Richardson, and H. L. Hunt playing cards on Murchison's plane, on their way to go fishing. *Dan Weiner* (1919–1959), for *Fortune*.

Gelatin silver print. Possibly Dallas, Dallas County, 1956. Collection of Sandra Weiner.

1950's

Collegiates at Rice University. *Unidentified photographer.*
Gelatin silver postcard montage. Houston, Harris County, 1952 or 1953. Collection of Bill Wright.

Disaster drill. The Hayes (firm active 1930s–1960s), for the *Dallas Times-Herald*. Modern gelatin silver print from the original safety negative. Dallas, Dallas County, about 1952. Texas/Dallas History and Archives Division, Dallas Public Library.

1950's

Pipeline under construction. *Russell Lee* (b. 1903). Gelatin silver print. Junction, Kimble County, 1950. Standard Oil (New Jersey) Collection, University of Louisville Photographic Archives.

"Campaigning on the court-house stairs—McKinney, Texas. Ralph Yarborough was running for governor—1954."
Russell Lee (b. 1903), for the *New York Times Magazine*.
Gelatin silver print. McKinney, Collin County, 1954. Collection of the photographer.

"Marion, Rose, and Thelma compare figures." *Grace Whitt* (1885–1958).
Gelatin silver print. Possibly west Texas, about 1950. Collection of Skeet McAuley.

"Skeet McAuley as a Christmas tree." *Thelma McAuley* (b. 1907).

Type C color print. Monahans, Ward County, 1957. Collection of Skeet McAuley.

1960's

Clover family portrait. *Grace Belden* (b. 1902).
Type C color print. Lubbock, Lubbock County, July 1965. Collection of Vernon and Hazel Clover.
Jeff Bedell, Phyllis Marotta, Carol Clover, and Paul Clover.

Clover family portrait. *Vernon Clover* (b. 1909).
Type C color print. Lubbock, Lubbock County, December 1968. Collection of Paul Clover.
The inscription on the back of the print reads: "Hazel Clover, Carol Clover, James Cox, Paul Clover, Tom Clover needing a shave and a haircut."

Children in Halloween costumes. *John F. "Doc" McGregor* (b. 1892).

Modern gelatin silver print from the original safety negative. Corpus Christi, Nueces County, Halloween, October 1963. Harry Ransom Humanities Research Center, University of Texas at Austin.

1960's

Dairy Queen. *Garry Winogrand* (1928–1984).
Gelatin silver print. San Marcos, Hays County, 1964. International Museum of Photography at the George Eastman House.

Swimming pig at Aquarena Springs. *Garry Winograd* (1928–1984).
Gelatin silver print. San Marcos, Hays County, 1964. Collection of Eileen Hale.

1960's

J. E. Wallis residence. *Henri Cartier-Bresson* (b. 1908), for *The Galveston that Was*.
Gelatin silver print. Galveston, Galveston County, about 1962. Magnum.

Sign and pick-up truck. *Lee Friedlander* (b. 1934).
Gelatin silver print. Unidentified location, 1965. Collection of the photographer.

The original seven astronauts with Stetsons and deputy sheriff's badges. *Unidentified photographer,* for the *Houston Chronicle.* Gelatin silver print. Houston, Harris County, July 4, 1962. *Houston Chronicle.*

1960's

Ralph Yarborough posing with Sally Greene. *Unidentified photographer*, for the *Gilmer Mirror*.
Gelatin silver print. Gilmer, Upshur County, 1964. *Gilmer Mirror*.

Yarborough was on a campaign trip through the state when this photograph was made at the courthouse where Sam Houston had spoken twice defending the Union.

"Stop that noise." *Richard Pipes* (b. 1936), for the *Amarillo Globe-News*.
Gelatin silver print. Amarillo, Potter County, 1960. Collection of the photographer.
During a campaign speech, John Kennedy was interrupted by the noise of a turbo-prop engine starting. Johnson and his wife, Lady Bird, shouted to stop the disturbance.

The Astros in the Astrodome. *Geoff Winningham* (b. 1943).
Gelatin silver print. Houston, Harris County, about 1964.
Collection of the photographer.

1960's

The Rodriguezes and their son. *Harry Forrest Annas* (1897–1980).
Modern gelatin silver print from the original safety negative. Lockhart,
Caldwell County, Fall 1968. Caldwell County Historical Commission and
Barker Texas History Center, University of Texas at Austin.
This photograph was made during a parents' night football game.

1960's

Dan Rather. *Unidentified photographer.* Gelatin silver print. Houston, Harris County, 1960. Wharton County Museum.

Rather, a native of Wharton, began his television career at the CBS affiliate station KHOU in Houston.

Lyndon Johnson taking the oath of office. *Unidentified photographer*, for United Press International.

Gelatin silver print. Dallas, Dallas County, November 22, 1963. United Press International/Bettmann Newsphotos.

Johnson, with Lady Bird and Jacqueline Kennedy standing beside him, is administered the oath of office by Federal District Judge Sarah T. Hughes aboard Air Force One.

1960's

Rush hour on the Gulf freeway. *Owen Johnson* (b. 1921), for the *Houston Post*.
Gelatin silver print. Houston, Harris County, 1965. Houston Metropolitan Research Center, Houston Public Library.

Spaghetti bowl. *The Hayes* (firm active 1930s–1960s), for the *Dallas Times-Herald*.
Modern gelatin silver print from the original safety negative. Dallas, Dallas County, about 1960. Texas/Dallas History and Archives Division, Dallas Public Library.

"Texaco." *Ed Ruscha* (b. 1937), from *Twenty-six Gasoline Stations*.
Gelatin silver print. Vega, Oldham County, 1962. Collection of the photographer.

Parking lot. *Lee Friedlander* (b. 1934).
Gelatin silver print. Dallas, Dallas County, 1969. Collection of the photographer.

Ground breaking for the Domed Stadium. *Unidentified photographer.* Gelatin silver print. Houston, Harris County, January 1962. Houston Sports Association.

Officials of the Houston Sports Association and Harris County Commissioners Court fired Colt .45s into the ground upon which the "Eighth Wonder of the World" was to be built. The baseball team was known as the Colt .45s; by the completion of the project, the team's name was changed to the Astros. Front row: George Kirksey, Earl Allen, Joe Cullinan, Craig Cullinan, Paul Richards, County Judge Bill Elliot, R. E. "Bob" Smith. Second row: Commissioners W. Kyle Chapman, V. V. Ramsey, Philip Sayers, E. A. "Squatty" Lyons, Jr.

1970's

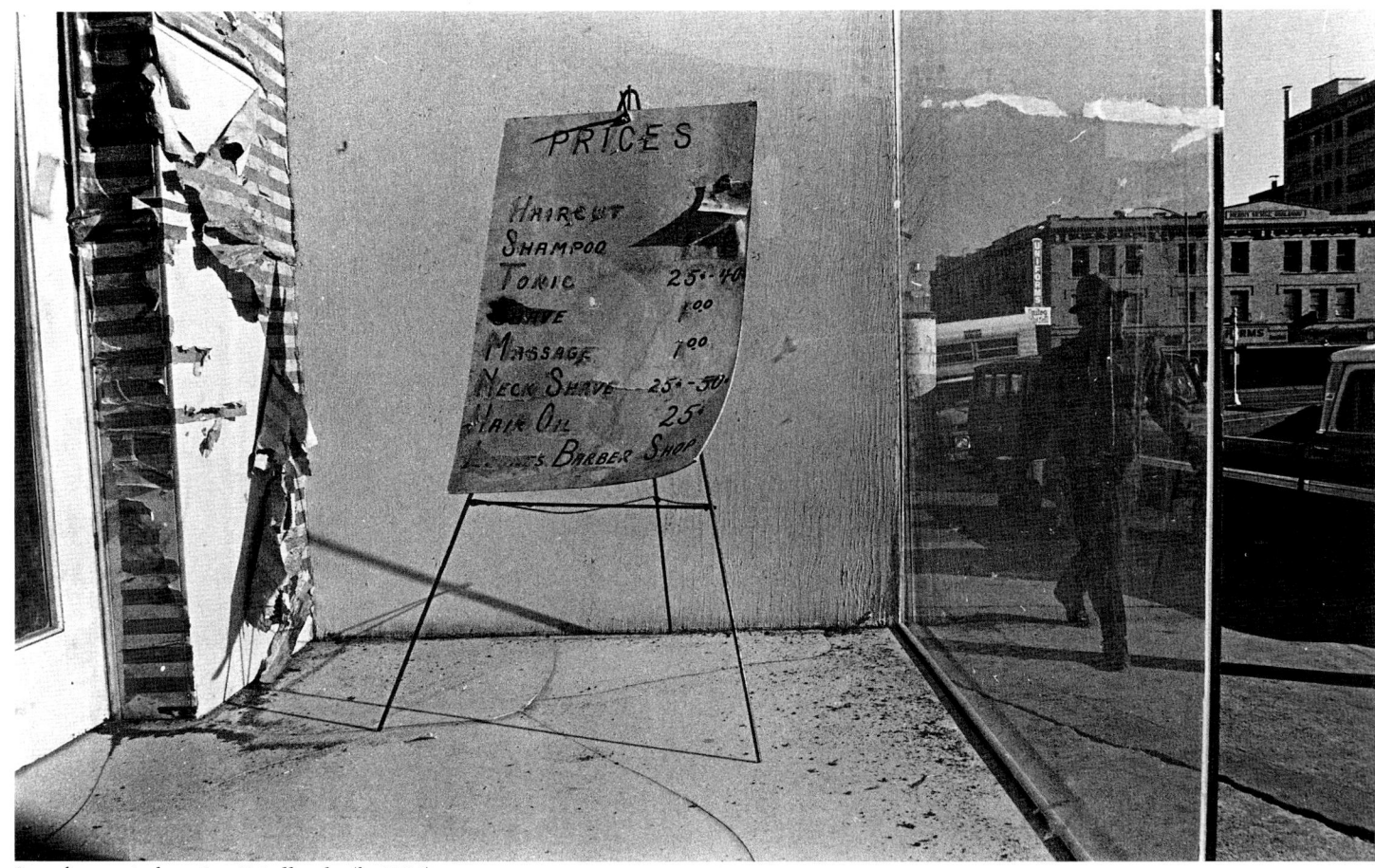

Storefront window. *Lee Friedlander* (b. 1934).
Gelatin silver print. Houston, Harris County, 1970.
Collection of the photographer.

Street scene. *Stephen Shore* (b. 1947). Ektacolor print. Presidio, Presicio County, 1975. Light Gallery.

1970's

"Grain elevators. Plainview, Texas, 1978." *Myron Wood* (b. 1921). Gelatin silver print. Plainview, Hale County, 1978. Collection of the photographer.

"LBJ Presidential Library and Gardener." *Alan Pogue* (b. 1946). Gelatin silver print. Austin, Travis County, 1972. Collection of the photographer.

Fat stock show. *Garry Winogrand* (1928–1984), from *Stock Photos: The Fort Worth Fat Stock Show and Rodeo.*
Gelatin silver print. Fort Worth, Tarrant County, 1980 or before. Collection of Eileen Hale.

Cowboy with *Wall Street Journal. Bert Brandt* (active 1970s).
Gelatin silver print. Houston, Harris County, about 1970. Houston Metropolitan Research Center, Houston Public Library.

"For God and Country." *Dennis Darling* (b. 1946).
Gelatin silver print. Vidor, Orange County, 1974. Collection of the photographer.

"Roloff." *Nancy E. Goldfarb* (b. 1951).

Gelatin silver print. Austin, Travis County, September 1973. Collection of the photographer.

Brother Roloff, a fundamentalist preacher unaffiliated with any Christian denomination, operated homes for delinquent children based on the principles of biblical indoctrination and corporal punishment. When the schools were ordered closed by the court for operating without a license and having substandard conditions, Roloff rallied the faithful for support, including prayers and gospel singing over the Attorney General and his staff at a public hearing. This photograph was made at a public assembly in Austin.

1970s

"Mr. Walker." *Tracy*, for *Gittings Studios, Dallas* (founded 1929).

Panalure print from the original color negative. Dallas, Dallas County, early 1970s. Gittings Corporation.

"Ms. Jordan." *Gittings Studios, Houston* (founded 1929).

Panalure print from the original color negative. Houston, Harris County, 1973. Gittings Corporation.

Barbara Jordan served in the Texas Senate from 1966 to 1972; she served in the United States House of Representatives from 1972 to 1978.

"Mr. Veselka. 'Now' Clean Hippie." *Blaker*, for *Gittings Studios, Houston* (founded 1929).

Panalure print from the original color negative. Houston, Harris County, early 1970s. Gittings Corporation.

"The recently out-of-fashion shots are the things people want to see least. They're not old enough to be history and recent enough to be a little embarrassing." Arthur Heitzman, for the Gittings Corporation.

1970s

The John Neely Bryan cabin, the old and new courthouses, and Reunion Center. *Phil Hollenbeck* (b. 1943).
Kodachrome. Dallas, Dallas County, 1978. Collection of the photographer.
John Neely Bryan was the founder of Dallas. He built this cabin in 1841 on the east bank of the Trinity River. The restored cabin has since been moved to its present site.

Site of the Kennedy assassination. *Daniel Barsotti* (b. 1950).
Gelatin silver print. Dallas, Dallas County, 1974. Collection of the photographer.
This photograph was made on November 22, exactly eleven years after John Kennedy's assassination.

"Break in the field." *Ken Light* (b. 1951), from *In the Fields*.
Gelatin silver print. Rio Grande Valley, 1979. Collection of the photographer.

"Nettie Featherston in the four room house she shares with her son."
Bill Ganzel (b. 1949), from *Dust Bowl Descent*.

Gelatin silver print. Lubbock, Lubbock County, August 1979.
Collection of the photographer.

Bill Ganzel photographed Nettie Featherston forty-one years after
Dorothea Lange made the photograph on page 206.
Featherston commented: "I never thought about living this long
[eighty-one years]. I just didn't think we'd survive. If you want to
know something, we're not living much better now than we did
then—as high as everything is."

1970's

Herding cattle with a helicopter. *Skeeter Hagler* (b. 1947), for the *Dallas Times-Herald*.
Gelatin silver print. Panhandle, 1980. Collection of the photographer.

Cowboy moving cattle out of a pen.
Skeeter Hagler
(b. 1947), for the
Dallas Times-Herald.
Gelatin silver print.
Panhandle, 1980.
Collection of the photographer.

1970's

Oveta Culp Hobby. *Joe Baraban* (b. 1945).
Ektachrome transparency. Houston, Harris County, 1978.
Collection of the photographer.
Oveta Culp Hobby (b. 1905) became publisher of the *Houston Post* in 1964. She was head of the Women's Army Corp during World War II, a secretary of the United States Department of Health, Education, and Welfare, and is a patron of education and the arts in Texas.

Prison laborers. *Danny Lyon* (b. 1942), from *Conversations with the Dead*.
Gelatin silver print. Midway, Madison County, 1968. Magnum.
Lyon's book documented the life and the people in the Texas Corrections facilities. The prisoners are at the Ferguson Prison farm.

Combine in wheat field. *Bill Ellzey* (b. 1945).
Kodachrome transparency. Near Perryton, Ochiltree County, about 1977.
Collection of the photographer.

1970's

Ellis County Courthouse. *Jim Dow* (b. 1942), from *Courthouse: A Photographic Document*.

Gelatin silver print. Waxahachie, Ellis County, 1977. Seagram's County Courthouse project; from a negative owned by the photographer.

Built between 1894 and 1897, the Ellis County courthouse is one of the outstanding examples of the design of architect James Riely Gordon.

Insurance office of R. B. Spacek. *Richard Greffe* (b. 1947).
Gelatin silver print. Fayetteville, about 1975. Collection of the photographer.

"Texas Aggie Fish." *Will van Overbeek* (b. 1955), from *Aggies: Life in the Corp of Cadets at Texas A&M*.

Gelatin silver print. College Station, Brazos County, 1979. Collection of the photographer.

"San Antonio Churchill versus Temple, Austin." *Geoff Winningham (b. 1943)*, from *Rites of Fall*.

Gelatin silver print. Austin, Travis County, 1976. Collection of the photographer.

Society ball. *Geoff Winningham* (b. 1943).
Gelatin silver print. Houston, Harris County, 1970s. Collection of the photographer.

Oblique view of the Texas coastline showing Houston and Galveston bay. *NASA.*

Type C color print. Galveston bay and environs, October 11–12, 1968. Texas Natural Resources Information System.

Optical center of this photograph is latitude 20°00″ N and longitude 94°00″ W. This photograph was taken by the crew of Apollo 7.

picture credits

All picture credits appear left to right, top to bottom.

Page

15	Collection of Oscar Backus. Austin, Texas.
18	Collection of Doris Houchen. Hugo, Oklahoma.
20	Collection of Doris Houchen. Hugo, Oklahoma.
44	Collection of Lawrence T. Jones. Austin, Texas.
44	Photograph Collection, Barker Texas History Center, University of Texas. Austin, Texas.
45	Photograph Collection, Barker Texas History Center, the University of Texas. Austin, Texas.
45	University of Texas Institute of Texan Cultures. San Antonio, Texas. 84-350.
46	Archives Division, Texas State Library. Austin, Texas. 1/136-1.
46	San Jacinto Museum of History Association. La Porte, Texas. L-1226.
47	Archives Division, Texas State Library. Austin, Texas. 1946/1-66.
48	Library of the Daughters of the Republic of Texas at the Alamo. San Antonio, Texas.
49	Smith County Historical Society Archives. Tyler, Texas.
49	Photograph Collection, Barker Texas History Center, University of Texas. Austin, Texas.
50	Archives Division, Texas State Library. Austin, Texas. 1/134-11.
50	La Retama Public Library. Corpus Christi, Texas.
51	Collection of Lawrence T. Jones. Austin, Texas.
51	Collection of Lawrence T. Jones. Austin, Texas.
52	Collection of Colleen Talmadge Clayborn. Palacios, Texas.
52	Prints and Photographs Division, Library of Congress. Washington, D.C.
53	Collection of Darnelle Vanghel. Austin, Texas.
53	Collection of Lawrence T. Jones. Austin, Texas.
56	San Jacinto Museum of History Association. La Porte, Texas. 14439.
56	Andrew W. George Papers, Barker Texas History Center, University of Texas. Austin, Texas.
57	Sophienberg Memorial Association Archives. New Braunfels, Texas. Faust album.

57	San Jacinto Museum of History Association. La Porte, Texas. 8389.
58	Fayette Heritage Museum/Archives. La Grange, Texas.
59	Collection of Lawrence T. Jones. Austin, Texas.
59	Collection of Lawrence T. Jones. Austin, Texas.
60	La Retama Public Library. Corpus Christi, Texas.
60	San Antonio Museum Association. San Antonio, Texas. 38-186-155-G.
61	Texas Collection, Baylor University. Waco, Texas. Gatesville, TX (12).
61	Texas Collection, Baylor University. Waco, Texas. Waco—Communications—Waco *Examiner*.
62	Fort Concho Museum. San Angelo, Texas.
63	Mazulla Collection, Amon Carter Museum. Fort Worth, Texas.
64	Amon Carter Museum. Fort Worth, Texas. 71.79/1.
65	University of Texas Institute of Texan Cultures. San Antonio, Texas. Original in the possession of Henry Hauschild. Victoria, Texas.
66	Austin History Center. Austin, Texas. PICA 13441.
67	Fort Concho Museum. San Angelo, Texas. R-968.
70	Collection of Lawrence T. Jones. Austin, Texas.
71	Collection of Lawrence T. Jones. Austin, Texas.
72	Fort Bend County Museum. Richmond, Texas. 73.90.11.
73	El Paso Public Library. El Paso, Texas.
74	Star of the Republic Museum. Washington-on-the-Brazos, Texas. C566.12.
74	Fayette Heritage Museum/Archives. La Grange, Texas. 80.106.24.
75	Texas Collection, Baylor University. Waco, Texas. Belton, TX (2).
75	San Antonio Museum Association. San Antonio, Texas. 75-101-26 G(3).
76-79	Fort Davis National Historic Site, Department of the Interior. Fort Davis, Texas. 1109, 1116, 1107, 1112, respectively.
80	Sophienberg Memorial Association Archives. New Braunfels, Texas. P-1030B.
81	San Antonio Museum Association. San Antonio, Texas. 77-48-12 G(14).
82	Amon Carter Museum. Fort Worth, Texas. 71.79/28.
83	University of Texas Institute of Texan Cultures. San Antonio, Texas. 83-477.
84	San Antonio Museum Association. San Antonio, Texas. 69-1-1 G(14).
84	Sophienberg Memorial Association Archives. New Braunfels, Texas. P-1015B.
85	San Antonio Museum Association. San Antonio, Texas. 80-7-171 Ga(27)a.
85	San Antonio Museum Association. San Antonio, Texas. 69-1-1 G(14).
86	San Antonio Museum Association. San Antonio, Texas. 41-46-435 G.
87	San Antonio Museum Association. San Antonio, Texas. 78-739-99 G(B1).
88	Rosenberg Library. Galveston, Texas.
89	Collection of Lawrence T. Jones. Austin, Texas.
92	Fort Concho Museum. San Angelo, Texas. R-993.
92	Harris County Heritage Society. Houston, Texas.
93	Sophienberg Memorial Association Archives. New Braunfels, Texas. Scheunemann album.
94	Ellis County Museum. Waxahachie, Texas. 249-H.
94	Dallas Historical Society. Dallas, Texas. A41207.
95	Rosenberg Library. Galveston, Texas. G 632.
95	Panhandle Plains Museum, West Texas State University. Canyon, Texas. Ph 1, 165/7.
96-97	Amon Carter Museum. Fort Worth, Texas. 79.41/108 and, 74 respectively.
98	Special Collections, University of Texas. Arlington, Texas.
98	San Jacinto Museum of History Association. La Porte, Texas. 3585C.
99	San Antonio Museum Association. San Antonio, Texas. 43.46.221 G.
99	Fort Concho Museum. San Angelo, Texas. 00.435.94.

100-101	Photograph Collection, Barker Texas History Center, University of Texas. Austin, Texas.	124	Panhandle Plains Museum, West Texas State University. Canyon, Texas. Ph 1, 273/8.
102	Harris County Heritage Society. Houston, Texas. 4:1894:01.	125	Panhandle Plains Museum, West Texas State University. Canyon, Texas. Ph 1, 260/81.
103	Sophienberg Memorial Association Archives. New Braunfels, Texas. P2012C.	126	Southwest Collection, Texas Tech University. Lubbock, Texas. 1980-120-17.
104-105	Texas Collection, Baylor University. Waco, Texas. Crush, TX (3).	127	Fort Concho Museum. San Angelo, Texas. R-780.
106	Midland County Museum. Midland, Texas.	127	San Antonio Museum Association. San Antonio, Texas. 50-13-379 G(12).
106	Smith County Historical Society Archives. Tyler, Texas.	128	Panhandle Plains Museum, West Texas State University. Canyon, Texas. Ph 1, 727/9.
107	Dallas Historical Society. Dallas, Texas. A7878/L721-360 #63. From *Views in Texas*. By Henry Stark. (Saint Louis: Privately published, n.d.).	128	Panhandle Plains Museum, West Texas State University. Canyon, Texas. Ph 1, 2802/1b.
107	Fort Concho Museum. San Angelo, Texas. 00.435.93.	129	Fort Concho Museum. San Angelo, Texas. R-1065.
108	Dallas Historical Society. Dallas, Texas. A7878/L721-360 #249. From *Views in Texas*. By Henry Stark. (Saint Louis: Privately published, n.d.).	129	San Antonio Museum Association. San Antonio, Texas.
109	Encino Press. Austin, Texas. From *Views in Texas*. Photographs by Henry Stark and commentary by A. C. Greene. Austin: Encino Press, 1974.	130	Photograph Collection, Barker Texas History Center, University of Texas. Austin, Texas.
110,113	Photograph Collection, Barker Texas History Center, University of Texas. Austin, Texas.	130	Smith County Historical Society Archives. Tyler, Texas. Ph-732.
111-112	Prints and Photographs Division, Library of Congress. Washington, D.C.	131	Panhandle Plains Museum, West Texas State University. Canyon, Texas. Ph 1, 22/289.22.
114-115	Sam Houston Regional Library and Research Center. Liberty, Texas. P. Hardin Collection.	131	Fayette Heritage Museum/Archives. La Grange, Texas. 81.83.58.
116	Collection of E. W. Ahlrich. Lake Jackson, Texas. Negative 22.	132	Texas/Dallas History and Archives Division, Dallas Public Library. 83-3811.
117	Fort Concho Museum. San Angelo, Texas. R-811.	133	Rosenberg Library. Galveston, Texas. G-5214.
118	La Retama Public Library. Corpus Christi, Texas.	134	Prints and Photographs Division, Library of Congress. Washington, D.C. 32374A.
119	Taulman Collection, Barker Texas History Center, University of Texas. Austin, Texas. II-106.	135	Layland Museum. Cleburne, Texas. 319.
122	Erwin E. Smith Collection, Prints and Photographs Division, Library of Congress. Washington, D.C. S59-47.	136	Rosenberg Library. Galveston, Texas.
122	Wharton County Museum. Wharton, Texas.	136	Rosenberg Library. Galveston, Texas. G-1771, folder 3.3.
123	Texas and Dallas History Collection, Dallas Public Library. Dallas, Texas. 84-5/6.	137	Sam Houston Regional Library and Research Center. Liberty, Texas.
123	Harris County Heritage Society. Houston, Texas. 981.51.08.	137	Photograph Collection, Barker Texas History Center, University of Texas. Austin, Texas. Kuehne 151.
		138	*Uvalde Leader News*. Uvalde, Texas.
		138	Pollack-Capps Collection, Special Collections Division, University of Texas. Arlington, Texas.

credits

credits

139	Smith County Historical Society Archives. Tyler, Texas. Y2594.
139	Smith County Historical Society Archives. Tyler, Texas. Y2637.
140	Rosenberg Library. Galveston, Texas. G-90189, folder 1.
141	Frank Elkin Collection, Midland County Museum. Midland, Texas. Folder 28.
141	University of Texas Institute of Texan Cultures. San Antonio, Texas. 70-412.
142	Fort Concho Museum. San Angelo, Texas. 337-BB-2.
143	Erwin E. Smith Collection, Prints and Photographs Division, Library of Congress. Washington, D.C. LC-S6-151.
144	Fort Concho Museum. San Angelo, Texas. R-837.
145	Texas/Dallas History and Archives Division, Dallas Public Library. Dallas, Texas. 83-3813.
148	Erwin E. Smith Collection, Prints and Photographs Division, Library of Congress. Washington, D.C. S59-521.
149	Fort Concho Museum. San Angelo, Texas. R-759.
149	Panhandle Plains Museum, West Texas State University. Canyon, Texas. Ph 1, 1982-8/64C.
150	Texas Labor Archives, University of Texas. Arlington, Texas.
151	William Deming Hornaday Collection, Archives Division, Texas State Library. Austin, Texas. 1975/70-5070.
152	San Antonio Museum Association. San Antonio, Texas. 74-11-3.
152	Paul Strand Archive and Library, Silver Mountain Foundation. Millerton, New York.
153	Museum of New Mexico. Santa Fe, New Mexico. 78493.
154	Collection of Colleen Talmadge Claybourn. Palacios, Texas.
155	William Deming Hornaday Collection, Archives Division, Texas State Library. Austin, Texas 1975/70-5060.
156	Collection of Maxine Havens. Hamilton, Texas.
156	Fort Bend County Museum. Richmond, Texas. 71.15.3III.
157	Truman G. Blocker Jr. History of Medicine Collection, Moody Medical Library, University of Texas Medical Branch. Galveston, Texas.
157	Collection of Dorothy Louise Burns. Highlands, Texas.
158	Collection of Jimmy Adair. Cleburne, Texas.
158	University of Texas Institute of Texan Cultures. San Antonio, Texas. 83-412.
159	Texas Collection, Baylor University. Waco, Texas. Waco—Businesses—ALICO (8); Gildersleeve negative 1696.
159	Texas Collection, Baylor University. Waco, Texas. Waco—Streets—Austin Ave (6).
160	John E. Conner Museum, Texas A & I University. Kingsville, Texas. 73-33-24.
160	Schuchard Collection, Library of the Daughters of the Republic of Texas at the Alamo. San Antonio, Texas.
161	Colorado Historical Society. Denver, Colorado.
162-163	Panhandle Plains Museum, West Texas State University. Canyon, Texas. Ph 10, 2230/1.
164	Collection of H. C. Williams. Orange, Texas.
165	Midland County Museum. Midland, Texas.
166	Target Collection of American Photography, Museum of Fine Arts. Houston, Texas. 76.725.
167	Collection of E. W. Ahlrich. Lake Jackson, Texas. Negative 17.
167	Collection of E. W. Ahlrich. Lake Jackson, Texas. Negative 82.
168	William Deming Hornaday Collection, Archives Division, Texas State Library. Austin, Texas. 75/70-1483.
169	Fort Concho Museum. San Angelo, Texas. R-866.
169	Smith County Historical Society Archives. Tyler, Texas.
172	Fayette Heritage Museum/Archives. La Grange, Texas. 80.3.39.
172	Harris County Heritage Society. Houston, Texas. P977.72.2335.
173	Hemphill County Library. Canadian, Texas.
173	Evans Collection, Amon Carter Museum. Fort Worth, Texas. 31 fr 21A-23. Courtesy of Tim and Rita Evans, Fort Worth.
174	Harris County Heritage Society. Houston, Texas. P977.72.2357A.
175	Texas Collection, Baylor University. Waco, Texas. Waco—Businesses—Progress Laundry.
175	Collection of Carol Roark, Fort Worth.

176	Texas Memorial Museum, University of Texas. Austin, Texas. L-489-19.
176	Texas/Dallas History and Archives Division, Dallas Public Library. Dallas, Texas. 78-2/1311.
177	Sophienberg Memorial Association Archives. New Braunfels, Texas. Seidel OS, Box 2, 01142.
177	Oral History Program, East Texas State University. Commerce, Texas.
178	Tyrrell Historical Library. Beaumont, Texas.
179	Collection of H. C. Williams. Orange, Texas.
179	Layland Museum. Cleburne, Texas.
180	San Antonio Museum Association. San Antonio, Texas. 80-119-193 G(10).
181	Goldbeck Collection, Photography Collection, Harry Ransom Humanities Research Center, University of Texas. Austin, Texas. 420.
182-183	Goldbeck Collection, Photography Collection, Harry Ransom Humanities Research Center, University of Texas. Austin, Texas. 751-2.
184	Goldbeck Collection, Photography Collection, Harry Ransom Humanities Research Center, University of Texas. Austin, Texas. 854-A.
185	Fort Bend County Museum. Richmond, Texas. 72.93.132.
186	Collection of Skeet McAuley. Dallas, Texas.
186	Marfa–Presidio County Museum. Marfa, Texas.
187	Marfa–Presidio County Museum. Marfa, Texas.
187	Hemphill County Library. Canadian, Texas.
188	University of Texas Institute of Texan Cultures. San Antonio, Texas. 0174-D.
188	University of Texas Institute of Texan Cultures. San Antonio, Texas. 0388-A.
189	University of Texas Institute of Texan Cultures. San Antonio, Texas. 0483-C.
189	University of Texas Institute of Texan Cultures. San Antonio, Texas. 0238-A.
190	Goldbeck Collection, Photography Collection, Harry Ransom Humanities Research Center, University of Texas. Austin, Texas. S-1-E.
191	Sophienberg Memorial Association Archives. New Braunfels, Texas. Seidel OS, 01964, Box 2.
194	Rector Collection, Photography Collection, Harry Ransom Humanities Research Center, University of Texas. Austin, Texas. I-3.
195	Prints and Photographs Division, Library of Congress. Washington, D.C. LC-USF-34-32264.
196	Farm Security Administration Collection, Prints and Photographs Division, Library of Congress. Washington, D.C. LC-USF-34-32010.
196	David R. Godine Publishers. Boston, Massachusetts. From *Championship Pig: Great Moments in Everyday Life*. By Barbara Norfleet. (Boston: Godine, 1979.)
197	David R. Godine Publishers. Boston, Massachusetts. From *Championship Pig: Great Moments in Everyday Life*. By Barbara Norfleet. (Boston: Godine, 1979.)
197	David R. Godine Publishers. Boston, Massachusetts. From *Championship Pig: Great Moments in Everyday Life*. By Barbara Norfleet. (Boston: Godine, 1979.)
198	Texas/Dallas History and Archives Division, Dallas Public Library. Dallas, Texas. 84-9/2.
199	Texas/Dallas History and Archives Division, Dallas Public Library. Dallas, Texas. 81-00179.
200	University of Texas Institute of Texan Cultures. San Antonio, Texas. 0050-G.
200	University of Texas Institute of Texan Cultures. San Antonio, Texas.
201	National Archives. Washington, D.C. 69-N-12684C.
202	McGregor Collection, Photography Collection, Harry Ransom Humanities Research Center, University of Texas. Austin, Texas. 492.
202	Chalberg Collection, Austin History Center. Austin, Texas. C03648.
203	Collection of Jane Alexander Knapik. Uvalde, Texas.
205	Texas/Dallas History and Archives Division, Dallas Public Library. Dallas, Texas. 19-59-288.
205	Chalberg Collection, Austin History Center. Austin, Texas. C6442.
206	National Archives. Washington, D.C. 69-N-P-632.
206	Farm Security Administration Collection, Prints and

credits

credits

205 Photographs Division, Library of Congress, Washington, D.C. LC-USF-34-18266-D.

206 Farm Security Administration Collection, Prints and Photographs Division, Library of Congress, Washington, D.C. LC-USF-34-18266-D.

207 Farm Security Administration Collection, Prints and Photographs Division, Library of Congress, Washington, D.C. LC-USF-34-4055-E.

207 Texas Collection, Baylor University. Waco, Texas. Spearman, TX (1).

208 Farm Security Administration Collection, Prints and Photographs Division, Library of Congress, Washington, D.C. LC-USF-34-32086.

208 Farm Security Administration Collection, Prints and Photographs Division, Library of Congress, Washington, D.C. LC-USF-34-9819-E.

209 Houston Metropolitan Research Center, Houston Public Library. Houston, Texas. 154-27. Works Progress Administration Project 565-3-3.

209 Photograph Collection, Barker Texas History Center, University of Texas. Austin, Texas. 83-209.

210 Collection of the photographer, Fritz Henle. St. Croix, U.S. Virgin Islands.

210 Trlica Collection, Photography Collection, Harry Ransom Humanities Research Center, University of Texas. Austin, Texas. 980:072:216.

211 Carl Mydans, *LIFE* Magazine. New York, New York. Copyright Time Inc.

212 Farm Security Administration Collection, Prints and Photographs Division, Library of Congress, Washington, D.C. LC-USF-34-34488-D.

212 Farm Security Administration Collection, Prints and Photographs Division, Library of Congress, Washington, D.C. LC-USF-34-32542-D.

213 Farm Security Administration Collection, Prints and Photographs Division, Library of Congress, Washington, D.C. LC-USF-34-32957-D.

213 Farm Security Administration Collection, Prints and Photographs Division, Library of Congress, Washington, D.C. LC-USF-34-12488-M3.

214 Farm Security Administration Collection, Prints and Photographs Division, Library of Congress, Washington, D.C. LC-USF-34-32220-D.

215 Carl Mydans, *LIFE* Magazine. New York, New York. Copyright Time Inc. 8-C/P-20.

216 Farm Security Administration Collection, Prints and Photographs Division, Library of Congress, Washington, D.C. LC-USF-34-33117-D.

216-217 Collection of Charles W. Perini. Abilene, Texas.

218 Carl Mydans, *LIFE* Magazine. New York, New York. Copyright Time Inc. Set 1/7C2.

219 Bradley Photographers. Dallas, Texas.

220 Sophienberg Memorial Association Archives. New Braunfels, Texas. Seidel OS, Box 2, 01954.

223 Bradley Photographers. Dallas, Texas.

224 Smithers Collection, Photography Collection, Harry Ransom Humanities Research Center, University of Texas. Austin, Texas. 3744-B.

225 Harris County Heritage Society. Houston, Texas.

226 Toni Frissell Collection, Prints and Photographs Division, Library of Congress, Washington, D.C.

226 Leonard McCombe, *LIFE* Magazine. New York, New York. Copyright 1949 Time Inc. #29341. UL 8-22-49.

227 Farm Security Administration Collection, Prints and Photographs Division, Library of Congress, Washington, D.C. LC-USF-34-35456-D.

228 Farm Security Administration Collection, Prints and Photographs Division, Library of Congress, Washington, D.C. LC-USF-34-35601-D.

229 Standard Oil (New Jersey) Collection, University of Louisville Photographic Archives. Louisville, Kentucky. 26191.

230 Office of War Information Collection, Prints and Photographs Division, Library of Congress, Washington, D.C. LC-USW-3-25224-D.

230 Cornell Capa, *LIFE* Magazine. New York, New York. Copyright 1947 Time Inc. #26056 UL 4-5-48.

231 Standard Oil (New Jersey) Collection, University of Louisville Photographic Archives. Louisville, Kentucky. 30910.

232 Southwest Collection, Texas Tech University. Lubbock, Texas. SWCPC57(G) 693.

233	Martin Dies Papers, Sam Houston Regional Library and Research Center. Liberty, Texas.	246	Rosenberg Library. Galveston, Texas. G-9127, folder 1.
234	Collection of A. J. Potter, Howard's Studio. Pecos, Texas.	247	Standard Oil (New Jersey) Collection, University of Louisville Photographic Archives. Louisville, Kentucky. 57139.
234	Center for Creative Photography, University of Arizona. Tucson, Arizona. Photography by Edward Weston, copyright 1981 Arizona Board of Regents. TX41-A-2.	247	Southwest Collection, Texas Tech University. Lubbock, Texas. SWCPC57 (C) 199.
235	Southwest Collection, Texas Tech University. Lubbock, Texas. SWCPC57 (C) 30.	248	Standard Oil (New Jersey) Collection, University of Louisville Photographic Archives. Louisville, Kentucky. 24371.
235	*Corpus Christi Caller-Times*. Corpus Christi, Texas.	249	Texas/Dallas History and Archives Division, Dallas Public Library. Dallas, Texas. 76-1/30004.
236	Collection of Iris C. Davis. Austin, Texas.	250	Standard Oil (New Jersey) Collection, University of Louisville Photographic Archives. Louisville, Kentucky. 25178.
236	National Archives. Washington, D.C. 306-PS-50-4421.	250	Collection of A. J. Potter, Howard's Studio. Pecos, Texas.
237	Jimmie A. Dodd Collection, Barker Texas History Center, University of Texas. Austin, Texas. 3563.	251	Amon Carter Museum. Fort Worth, Texas. 83.32/4.
237	Southwest Collection, Texas Tech University. Lubbock, Texas. SWCPC57 (D) 258.	251	Standard Oil (New Jersey) Collection, University of Louisville Photographic Archives. Louisville, Kentucky. 26510.
238	Amon Carter Museum. Fort Worth, Texas. 80.23/1. Photography by Edward Weston used by permission, copyright 1981 the Arizona Board of Regents. Tucson, Arizona.	252	Goldbeck Collection, Photography Collection, Harry Ransom Humanities Research Center, University of Texas. Austin, Texas. C-71947-E.
239	Standard Oil (New Jersey) Collection, University of Louisville Photographic Archives. Louisville, Kentucky. 37848.	253	Standard Oil (New Jersey) Collection, University of Louisville Photographic Archives. Louisville, Kentucky. 57267.
240	Sophienberg Memorial Association Archives. New Braunfels, Texas. Seidel OS, Box 42.1, 3211/42.	254	Rosenberg Library. Galveston, Texas. G-6563, folder 1.
240	Pan American Union Collection, Prints and Photographs Division, Library of Congress, Washington, D.C. PR6(AA), CN18C, L-420.	254	Amon Carter Museum. Fort Worth, Texas. 81.35/1.
241	Texas/Dallas History and Archives Division, Dallas Public Library. Dallas, Texas. 76-1/4819A.	255	*Texas Monthly*. Austin, Texas. Courtesy of Gittings Corporation. Dallas, Texas.
242	Pan American Union Collection, Prints and Photographs Division, Library of Congress, Washington, D.C. PR6(AA), CN18C, L-420.	256	Rosenberg Library. Galveston, Texas. G-68624, folder 1.
243	Office of War Information Collection, Prints and Photographs Division, Library of Congress. Washington, D.C. LC-USW-3-30950-D.	257	Rosenberg Library. Galveston, Texas. G-68625, folder 4.
		258	Standard Oil (New Jersey) Collection, University of Louisville Photographic Archives. Louisville, Kentucky. 64123.
244	Amon Carter Museum. Fort Worth, Texas. 79.134/1 Copyright 1977/Amon Carter Museum.	259	Leonard McCombe, *LIFE* Magazine. New York, New York. Copyright 1949 Time Inc.
245	Ansel Adams Publishing Rights Trust. Carmel, California. All rights reserved.	262	Bradley Photography. Dallas, Texas.
246	Cornell Capa, *LIFE* Magazine. New York, New York. Copyright 1947 Time Inc. #22681 UL 2-3-47.	262	Texas/Dallas History and Archives Division, Dallas Public Library. Dallas, Texas. 76-1/2244.1.
		263	Texas/Dallas History and Archives Division, Dallas Public Library. Dallas, Texas. 76-1/10572.1.
		263	Collection of the photographer, Robert Frank.
		264	Metropolitan Research Center, Houston Public Library.

Houston, Texas. 114-1404.

265 Collection of the photographer, Eliot Porter. Courtesy of Scheinbaum and Russek Gallery. Santa Fe, New Mexico. 810-50-29.

266 Clarence John Laughlin Collection, Historic New Orleans Collection. 533 Royal Street, New Orleans, Louisiana. CJL Negative number 12913. Copyright 1984 Historic New Orleans Collection.

267 Texas/Dallas History and Archives Division, Dallas Public Library. Dallas, Texas. 81-00425.

268 Collection of the photographer, Robert Frank.

268 Collection of the photographer, Russell Lee. Austin, Texas.

269 Heritage Museum of Falfurrias. Falfurrias, Texas.

270 Commerce Local History Collection, Commerce Public Library. Commerce, Texas.

271 Texas/Dallas History and Archives Division, Dallas Public Library. Dallas, Texas. 76-1/6200.1

271 David R. Godine, Publishers. Boston, Massachusetts. From *Champion Pig: Great Moments in Everyday Life*. By Barbara Norfleet. (Boston: Godine, 1979.)

272 Collection of Sandra Weiner. New York, New York.

272 Gift of the Pablo Frank Trust, Museum of Fine Arts, Houston. Houston, Texas. ACC:82.478. Courtesy of Robert Frank.

273 Harris County Heritage Society. Houston, Texas. P977.72.2430.

273 Texas/Dallas History and Archives Division, Dallas Public Library. Dallas, Texas. 84-913.

274 Biggs Collection, Texas/Dallas History and Archives Division, Dallas Public Library. Dallas, Texas. 81-00144.

275 Collection of Sandra Weiner. New York, New York.

276 Collection of Bill Wright. Abilene, Texas.

277 Hayes Collection, Texas/Dallas History and Archives Division, Dallas Public Library. Dallas, Texas. 76-1/16502.1.

278 Standard Oil (New Jersey) Collection, University of Louisville Photographic Archives. Louisville, Kentucky. 67117.

279 Collection of the photographer, Russell Lee. Austin, Texas.

280 Collection of Skeet McAuley. Dallas, Texas.

281 Collection of Skeet McAuley. Dallas, Texas.

284 Collection of Vernon and Hazel Clover. Plano, Texas.

284 Collection of Paul Clover. Austin, Texas.

284 *Houston Chronicle*. Houston, Texas.

285 McGregor Collection, Photography Collection, Harry Ransom Humanities Research Center, University of Texas. Austin, Texas. 1-31-63.

286 The International Museum of Photography at the George Eastman House. Rochester, New York. Courtesy of Eileen Hale. Los Angeles, California.

287 Collection of Eileen Hale. Los Angeles, California.

288 Magnum. New York, New York. From *The Galveston that Was*. Text by Howard Barnstone; photographs by Henri Cartier-Bresson and Ezra Stoller. (New York: Macmillan, 1979.)

288 Collection of the photographer, Lee Friedlander. New City, New York.

290 *Gilmer Mirror*. Gilmer, Texas.

290 Collection of the photographer, Richard Pipes. Albuquerque, New Mexico.

291 Caldwell County Historical Commission. Lockhart, Texas. Negatives now at Barker Texas History Center, University of Texas. Austin, Texas.

291 Collection of the photographer, Geoff Winningham. Houston, Texas.

292 Wharton County Museum. Wharton, Texas.

293 United Press International/Bettman Newsphotos. New York, New York. 1402669.

294 Metropolitan Research Center, Houston Public Library. Houston, Texas. 157-622.

294 Hayes Collection, Texas/Dallas History and Archives Division, Dallas Public Library. Dallas, Texas. 76-1/29964.5.

295 Collection of the photographer, Ed Ruscha. Hollywood, California. From *Twentysix Gasoline Stations*. By Ed Ruscha. (Alhambro, California: Cunningham Press, 1962.)

296 Collection of the photographer, Lee Friedlander. New City, New York.

297 Houston Sports Association. Houston, Texas.

300	Collection of the photographer, Lee Friedlander. New City, New York.
301	Light Gallery. New York, New York.
302	Collection of the photographer, Myron Wood. Colorado Springs, Colorado. 2786-2.
302	Collection of the photographer, Alan Pogue. Austin, Texas.
303	Brandt Collection, Houston Metropolitan Research Center, Houston Public Library. Houston, Texas.
303	Collection of Eileen Hale. Los Angeles, California. From *Stock Photos: The Fort Worth Fat Stock Show and Rodeo*. By Garry Winogrand. (Austin: University of Texas Press, 1980.)
304	Collection of the photographer, Dennis Darling. Austin, Texas.
305	Collection of the photographer, Nancy E. Goldfarb. Austin, Texas.
306	Gittings Corporation. Dallas, Texas. 8031NMN/#2.
306	Gittings Corporation. Dallas, Texas. HL26251/#5.
307	Gittings Corporation. Dallas, Texas. HL29857/#1.
308	Collection of the photographer, Phil Hollenbeck. Dallas, Texas.
308	Collection of the photographer, Daniel Barsotti. Dallas, Texas.
309	Collection of the photographer, Bill Ganzel. Lincoln, Nebraska. From *Dust Bowl Descent*. By Bill Ganzel. (Lincoln: University of Nebraska Press, 1984.)
309	Collection of the photographer, Ken Light. Vallejo, California. From *In the Fields*. Photographs by Ken Light, Roger Minick, and Reesa Tansey; historical essay by Paul Schuster Taylor and Anne Loftis. (Oakland, California: Harvest Press, 1982.)
310	Collection of the photographer, Skeeter Hagler. Dallas, Texas.
311	Collection of the photographer, Skeeter Hagler. Dallas, Texas.
312	Collection of the photographer, Joe Baraban. Houston, Texas.
313	Collection of the photographer, Bill Ellzey. Telluride, Colorado. 20/109. Copyright 1977 Bill Ellzey.
313	Magnum. New York, New York. From *Conversations with the Dead*. By Danny Lyon. (New York: Holt, Rinehart, & Winston, 1971.)
314	Seagram's County Courthouse Project, from a negative owned by the photographer, Jim Dow. Belmont, Massachusetts. From *Courthouse: A Photographic Document*. By Richard Pare. (New York: Horizon, 1978.)
314	Collection of the photographer, Richard Greffe. Austin, Texas.
315	Collection of the photographer, Will van Overbeek. Austin, Texas. From *Aggies: Life in the Corp of Cadets at Texas A&M*. By Will van Overbeek. (Austin: Texas Monthly Press, 1982.)
315	Collection of the photographer, Geoff Winningham. Houston, Texas. From *Rites of Fall*. By Geoff Winningham. (Austin: University of Texas Press, 1979.)
316	Collection of the photographer, Geoff Winningham. Houston, Texas.
317	Texas Natural Resources Information System. Austin, Texas. Courtesy of NASA. AS7-7-1870.